Root Vegetables

Marshall Cavendish London & New York

Edited by Robin Wood

Published by Marshall Cavendish Books Limited
58 Old Compton Street
London W1V 5PA

© Marshall Cavendish Limited 1977, 1978, 1979

This material has previously appeared in the Marshall Cavendish partwork *Grow Your Own*.

First printing 1979

Printed in Great Britain
by Henry Stone and Son Limited
Banbury

ISBN 0 85685 486 7

Introduction

Among the popular root vegetables featured in this book are some of the most regularly used of all garden crops—including onions, potatoes and carrots—and one of the ugliest, least grown, and yet most nutritious and easily cultivated of vegetables—the Jerusalem artichoke. All give a welcome year-round return. And when harvested fresh from your garden, they are both wholesome and delicious, and a boon to any cook.

Each chapter deals with a single crop, and gives you the detailed and comprehensive instructions you need to grow it to perfection. We begin with the basic facts about the crop—sowing to harvesting time, size and yield—to help you to plan your garden. Three types of symbols, explained below, are used to give an at-a-glance guide to the nature of the crop.

Then we give full details, with clear step-by-step illustrations, on preparing the soil, sowing the crop, caring for it during growth, harvesting and storing, and even preparing your prize products for exhibition.

Of particular value are the separate sections on identifying and combating the pests and diseases that threaten your products, as well as the guides to the most popular varieties available for you to choose from.

Practical both in size and format, *Root Vegetables* will soon have earned its place on your gardening shelf.

🍠 low yield	🎵 minimum effort	◗ crops in three months or less
🍠🍠 medium yield	🎵🎵 needs more care	◗ crops in 4–12 months
🍠🍠🍠 high yield	🎵🎵🎵 requires special attention	◗ crops in over 12 months

Contents

Root Vegetables

Beetroot

Beta vulgaris (fam. *Chenopodiaceae*)
Half-hardy biennial, grown as an **annual.**
Sowing to harvesting time: round and intermediate types 8-10 weeks; long types about 19 weeks.
Size: plants about 30 cm (1′) tall, swollen roots between 2.5 cm (1″) and 9 cm (3½″) in diameter, according to form and variety at picking time.
Yield: round and oval types, about 40 roots per 3 m (10′) row; long beet about 20 roots per 3 m (10′) row.

Beet is a fairly straightforward vegetable to raise, and one which has long been popular with amateur growers. It has so many uses in the kitchen that you are never likely to waste any of the crop—as well as adding rich colour and flavour to soups, salads and chutneys it is excellent served as a hot vegetable, and its high sugar content makes it a very good base for home-made wine.

The most common type of beet is round (sometimes called globe, or ball) and deep carmine in colour. These are usually eaten in salads, when they are young and tender, but they can also be grown as a maincrop and stored. There are two other shapes—oval (known as intermediate, or tankard) and long. Long beet is not often grown today, partly because it is less sweet and succulent than the round varieties, and partly because the roots are so large that they will not fit into today's modern saucepans. It does, however, store well and is good for exhibition work.

Although most varieties of beet are red, white and golden beets are now available to the amateur. These are round shaped, and their main advantage over red beet is that they do not 'bleed' in salads. They are doubly useful in the kitchen, because the leaves can be cooked and served like spinach.

By planting several varieties and giving some form of cloche protection in early spring, you can easily have a good supply of beetroot all the year round. A native of the Mediterranean region, it is not frost hardy in colder climates. Winter beetroot should be lifted before the first frosts, and stored until you need them.

Suitable site and soil

Globe beets are reasonably tolerant of soil conditions, and will grow in any well drained soil which does not dry out in summer. However, light sandy soils are ideal for all types of beet, particularly long varieties, which need a deep sandy loam to grow well. Select a site that is open and sunny for best results.

Begin preparing heavy soils in late autumn; light soils can be prepared early in spring. If the soil is very heavy, dig in plenty of half rotted straw or peat to lighten it. Coarse sand can also be used. Double dig if you are preparing the bed for long beet, otherwise digging to about 17.5 cm (7″) is adequate. Remove all weeds and their roots. If you have dug the soil in the autumn, leave it rough so that winter weather will break it down and make it more friable. If the soil is stony, remove as many as possible, because the roots should be able to grow and penetrate the soil without obstructions which may deform them.

Avoid adding fresh manure when preparing a bed for beet, or you are likely to get forked, mis-shapen roots. Ideally, beet should be grown on part of the vegetable plot which was manured the previous season; beets can sensibly follow celery, peas or runner beans. However, because of beet's maritime associations, seaweed can be added to the soil, provided it is mixed into the bottom spit in autumn.

If the soil has an acid reaction, supply lime sometime in mid-winter sufficient to make the pH neutral or very slightly alkaline. In spring, just before sowing, apply a compound fertilizer at the rate of 60 g per sq m (2 oz per sq yd), but only if seaweed was not added, and rake the soil level.

Sowing

Although beets are reasonably hardy, seedlings can be damaged by heavy frost. If the seedlings are not killed outright, they are liable to be stunted and produce seeds without forming an edible root. There is no point in sowing before mid-spring, unless you live in a very mild area or can give cloche protection. For spring sowings, try to make a point of using bolt-resistant varieties, as beet has a great tendency to run to seed in dry and/or hot conditions.

Round beets for salads should be sown

1. **Prepare heavy soils in autumn, and leave rough over winter; light sandy soils can be prepared in the spring.**

2. **Test the soil; if it is acid, apply lime at a rate to give a neutral or slightly alkaline reaction.**

3. **In spring, work the soil to a fine tilth; prepare drills 30 cm (1′) apart and 2.5 cm (1″) deep.**

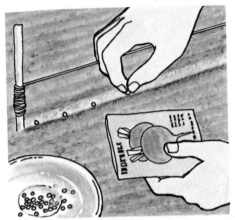

1. Sow seed clusters 5 cm (2″) apart, in small batches, from mid-spring to mid-summer.

2. After sowing fill in the drills with fine soil, and rake the bed lightly to give an even surface.

3. Thin the seedlings as soon as they are large enough to handle; leave one at each station.

4. Thin again, giving a final spacing of 10 cm (4″) for round varieties, and 15 cm (6″) for long varieties.

in small batches until mid-summer. By monthly successional sowing, you will be provided with a continual supply of fresh young roots. Beets to be used for storage should be sown in early summer. Do not sow them earlier in the season, or they will have grown too coarse and woody by the time lifting starts in autumn.

Beet seeds are grouped in capsules, or clusters, each containing four or five seeds. Seeds, if properly stored, will maintain their viability for four years. To hasten germination, soak the seeds in water for a few hours before sowing. The average seed packet will contain enough seeds for several rows, so only soak as many as you intend to use immediately.

Sow each seed cluster 5 cm (2″) apart in rows 30 cm (1′) apart. Make the drills 2.5 cm (1″) deep, and after sowing fill in the drill with soil. Rake lightly to give a fine surface and water if the weather is dry. Germination should be within 12-24 days of sowing. When the seedlings appear, there will be clusters of them at each station. Remove all but the strongest as soon as they are large

1. Beetroot needs a steady supply of water while it is growing, during the mid and late summer particularly.

2. Hoe as necessary between rows, being very careful not to damage the roots with the blade of the hoe.

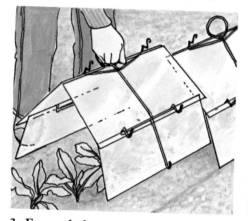

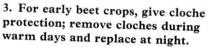

3. For early beet crops, give cloche protection; remove cloches during warm days and replace at night.

4. When harvesting, lift the roots with a fork to avoid damaging the long tap root.

enough to handle. Thin them again, when they are between 2.5-7.5 cm (1-3″) tall for round and intermediate varieties, and 15 cm (6″) tall for long varieties, giving a spacing of 10 cm (4″) and 15 cm (6″) respectively.

Care and development

The cultivation needs of beet are moderate. For the best flavour, beets should grow quickly, otherwise tasteless, cracked, mis-shapen and tough roots will result. This means the plants must have a steady supply of water at the roots, especially during mid and late summer.

If you have thoroughly removed all weeds when preparing the soil, you should have little trouble with weeds while the crops are growing. Once the plants are established, they produce thick foliage which suppresses the weeds. If weeding is necessary, however, hand weed between the plants to avoid damaging the roots; light hoeing between rows is all right if you are very careful and keep well away from the beets.

Beetroot crops are best when grown quickly and given a steady supply of water.

Because beet in its natural state grows near the sea, a light application of agricultural (common or rock) salt is useful. Apply in early or mid-summer, at the rate of 30 g per sq m (1 oz per sq yd) and fork it in lightly.

Birds are much attracted to seedlings and some protection is essential. You can protect the rows with netting, pea guards or black cotton thread twined around and through the leaves.

Container growing

Choose round varieties for container growing. Large tubs are most suitable but, if using pots, the smallest useful size is 30 cm (1′). Fill the bottom 5 cm (2″) of the container with small pieces of broken bricks, pieces of flower pot or hardcore to provide drainage. Fill the container with John Innes potting compost No 3 mixture to within 5 cm (2″) of the rim. Then sprinkle the seeds thinly over the surface and cover with another 2.5 cm (1″) of compost. Water well, using a fine rose on the watering can. Thin the seedlings to allow enough room for them to develop, leaving only eight plants in a

30 cm (1′) diameter pot. Water frequently in warm weather.

Forcing

Although you may have stored enough beetroot from the previous year's crop to last through spring, fresh early beet is a real treat and one which is easy to produce. Round varieties are the most suitable for growing under cloches or in frames. Tent and tunnel cloches will accommodate a single row; wider sorts of cloches will take two or three rows, spaced 17.5 cm (7″) apart. Sow thinly in early spring in seed drills 2.5 cm (1″) deep. Thin as soon as the seedlings are large enough to handle to 5 cm (2″) apart; make sure they never run short of water.

After germination, provided that the days are not excessively cold, open the frames or cloches slightly to admit air. Close when night temperatures fall below about 10°C (50°F). Remove the frame lid or cloches entirely on days when temperatures average above 16 C (60°F), but replace in the evening if frost threatens.

Harvesting and storing

Round and intermediate varieties should be ready for pulling when they are about 2.5 cm (1″) in diameter, about eight weeks after they are sown. These first pullings are in fact a form of thinning, as the remaining beets will have room to grow larger. For this reason, try to pick evenly over the rows, so the rest of the crop is reasonably spaced. These first pullings will be very tender, and useful for salads. Continue pulling more beet as and when needed, until they reach 6-7.5 cm (2½-3″) in diameter. Try to pull the roots as soon as they are fully mature. Once the foliage begins to lose its fresh look and goes limp, it means that growing has stopped and the plants are best harvested immediately.

Maincrops should be ready for harvesting from early autumn, continuing for about two months; this includes the long varieties for winter storing. Loosen the roots with a fork or spade and then lever out; it is best not to wrench the plants out by pulling the leaves. The one exception is the variety *Cook's Delight*, which grows with most of the root out of the ground. These roots will come out quite easily when pulled by the leaves.

Do not cut off the leaves, but twist them off about 5 cm (2″) above the crown. This is to avoid breaking the skin and subsequent bleeding, which would detract from the flavour and colour. Then shake the root to remove adhering soil. The leaves of some varieties can be eaten fresh or cooked as greens.

All beets can be stored for future use; if properly stored they will keep until the first of the following year's crop is ready for lifting. Although some varieties are slightly more frost hardy than others, beet can be damaged by severe frost. For this reason, unless you live in a very mild area, you should harvest the crop no later

To store in boxes, line the bottom with sand; place a layer of beetroot on sand, and cover with sand or peat; continue the layers until the box is filled.

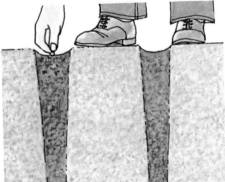

1. Make holes with a crowbar 1.05m (3′6″) deep, and 30 cm (1′) apart. Leave 45 cm (1′6″) between rows.

2. Fill the holes with John Innes potting compost; press the compost in firmly, and sow seeds in the top.

than the first touch of autumn frost. If you do leave them in the ground protect them from frost with a layer of clean straw or bracken. Select a dry day for lifting and be careful not to damage the roots in any way. Damaged, diseased or bruised roots cannot be stored as they may rot and quickly infect the others.

If your crop is moderate-sized, you can store it in boxes. Line the bottom of the container with 5 cm (2″) of sand or peat; then lay beetroots on the bottom, not touching each other. Add a 2.5 cm (1″) layer of peat or sand and another layer of beet and so on until the box is

fully packed. Then store the boxes in a cool, dry place such as a garden shed, outhouse, garage or cellar. If the storage conditions are too warm or moist, the roots may continue to grow or rot may set in and spoil the crop.

If your harvest is a large one, you can build a clamp, similar to a potato clamp, for beetroot storage (see POTATO).

Exhibition tips

Try to time beetroot sowing so the crop will be just ready for exhibiting; roots which are premature or those which are old and woody will not win prizes. For early summer shows, long varieties should be sown in late winter outdoors with glass protection. Globe varieties should be sown in mid-spring for mid-summer shows, and in late spring for late summer shows.

Globe roots for show can be selected from ordinary crops, and no special cultivation is needed. Long varieties for show are best planted in holes made by a crowbar, 30 cm (1′) apart, 1.05 m (3′6″) deep, in rows 45 cm (18″) apart, filled with John Innes potting compost. Press compost in firmly, leaving a 2.5 cm (1″) depression in the top, in which the seeds are sown. Thin out to one strong plant as soon as the seedlings are large enough to handle, and continue cultivating as for normal crops.

Brian Furner

Round varieties are the best sort for container growing; keep them well watered.

3. Before the show, trim back leaf stalks to 7.5 cm (3″) and cut off tiny rootlets with a sharp knife.

When it is time to lift the roots, either round or long, you must take care not to damage the tap root. Do not pull the plants out of the ground by their leaves; it is much better to lift them with a fork or spade.

For both varieties, remove the tiny side rootlets with a sharp knife. Cut off all the outer leaves cleanly; leave 7.5 cm (3″) of leaf stalk from the inner leaves. Wash the roots in cold water to remove any soil adhering, but do not scrub them. Dry the roots and wrap them in paper until the show.

Very large roots are not necessarily prizewinners; it is best to select medium-sized roots which have good colour and are free from blemishes, pale inner rings and damage. The tap root should still be intact. Globe varieties should be symmetrical, smooth skinned, and about the size of a tennis ball. Long varieties should taper evenly from the shoulder to a single tap root. Do not enter roots which are forked or have gall marks, or roots which bulge too much in the middle.

Long varieties are usually shown in a flat basket on a bed of parsley; round varieties can be piled, pyramid shape, in a round basket. Just before judging, spray the beets with a fine mist of water, to make them as visually appetizing as possible.

Pests & Diseases

Mangold flies (beet leaf miner): the maggots of the mangold fly damage the leaves of beet by feeding on them; they mine through the leaves and produce large, pale brown blisters. The worst damage is done when the plants are young; in bad attacks the plants may be killed outright. Infested plants will be stunted; leaves will turn completely brown, wither and die. Pick off and burn all infested leaves. If it is a severe attack, spray the remainder with trichlorphon. Remember to allow the specified interval to elapse between treatment and harvesting. It is a good idea to apply a quick-acting fertilizer to attacked crops to give them a chance to make fresh top growth.

Beet carrion beetle: the grub and adult stage of this black beetle feed on the tender leaves for about three weeks in spring; in severe attacks, the plants may be killed. In general it is not a serious pest, and clean cultivation and frequent hoeing are the best preventive measures. If your plants are attacked, spray with derris as soon as the pests are seen and repeat as necessary.

Swift moth: the dirty white caterpillars of the swift moth can be very destructive; they live in the soil and feed on the roots. Hoe and fork lightly round the beets

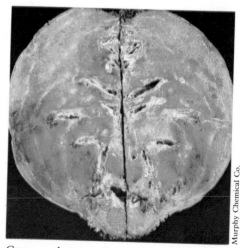

Crown or heart rot is an indication of boron deficiency; roots become cankered and black.

9

regularly if the soil is infested; this will kill some caterpillars and expose some to insect-eating birds. Because they also feed on the roots of many weeds, such as docks, try to keep your garden weed free. If the attack is severe, try trichlorphon.

Scab: this fungal disease is usually associated with limey soils. Symptoms are small marks or sunken pits; occasionally they are raised above the level of the skin. The small markings will gradually increase in size, until the whole root is disfigured. Although plants are rarely killed by scab, beetroot covered with scab is less pleasant to eat. The best preventive measure is to correct the pH of the soil before planting. You can also dig in green manure, lawn mowings, or moist peat just before sowing as an additional precaution.

Damping off: this is a fungal disease associated with wet, overcrowded conditions. Infected seedlings will collapse at ground level and die; roots of infected plants are usually discoloured reddish-brown. The best preventive measure is to avoid overcrowding the seedlings; thin as soon as they are big enough to handle. If the seedlings are attacked, remove and destroy the infected plants and spray the remainder with Cheshunt compound, captan or zineb.

Violet root rot: this is a very serious

Crown gall is a bacterial infection which causes bumps to form on the sides of roots.

fungal disease. It is soil borne, and infected roots when lifted will show webs of violet strands enmeshing them. The above-ground symptoms of violet root rot are wilting and yellow leaves, but to be absolutely sure you must dig up and inspect the root of the suspect plant. Unfortunately, there is no chemical cure; grub up and destroy infected plants. Do not replant the site with beets, or any other vegetable susceptible to violet root rot for three years. Parsnip, carrots, asparagus and potatoes are particularly susceptible, so avoid planting them if the soil is infected.

Beet rust: this is a less severe fungal infection, the symptoms of which are small red-brown spots on the under surfaces of the leaves. It is most likely to be seen in autumn and is unlikely to

---

GUIDE TO BEET TROUBLES

Symptoms	Probable causes
Brown, withered and blistered leaves	Mangold fly
Leaves eaten	Beet carrion beetle
Roots eaten	Swift moth caterpillar
Small marks or sunken pits on roots; roots disfigured	Scab
Seedlings collapse and die	Damping off
Yellow stunted leaves; roots surrounded by webs of violet fungus	Violet root rot
Small brown spots on leaves	Beet rust
Large hollow cavities in roots	Crown gall
Blackened root and central leaves	Boron deficiency
Pale areas between leaf veins which eventually turn brown and die	Magnesium deficiency
Yellow blotches on leaves; leaves curled upwards	Manganese deficiency

Murphy Chemical Co.

These beetroots are infected with scab, a fungal disease associated with limey soils

Ministry of Agriculture, Fisheries & Food

Beets suffering from manganese deficiency have leaves which are discoloured or curled.

cause much trouble. Pick off and burn infected leaves as soon as you see them; if the disease is severe, spray the remainder with captan or zineb. Spray again a fortnight later.

Crown gall: this is a bacterial infection usually associated with badly drained soils. The bacteria enter the plant through a wound, perhaps made by an insect or damage from a hoe or fork. Once inside the roots, their attack results in the formation of large bumps on the sides of the roots. It is not a serious infection, although the roots may be slightly stunted and less appetizing. However, many other root plants can be seriously attacked and damaged, so infected roots should be dug up and burned as soon as seen. The best preventive measure is to correct any drainage problems before the crop is planted; also avoid damaging the roots during routine cultivation.

Boron deficiency: this is most likely to occur on light sandy soils in dry weather; plants growing on very limey soils are also vulnerable. The symptoms of boron deficiency are commonly called crown or heart rot; the central leaves die back and become blackened, and the roots may turn black on the inside and be cankered on the outside. To correct boron deficiency, mulch with plenty of garden compost, well-rotted manure, leaf-mould, or seaweed, or apply liquid seaweed fertilizer at the recommended rate.

Magnesium deficiency: magnesium is one of the constituents of chlorophyll, and if beetroot is lacking magnesium, pale areas will appear between the leaf veins. Eventually these discoloured areas turn brown and die. The deficiency is most likely to occur on very acid or very limey soils, but in general it is seldom encountered. One or more foliar sprays at two-weekly intervals with magnesium sulphate (Epsom salts) at the rate of 60 g in 4.5 L of water (2 oz in 1 gal) may be tried. A good mulch of well-rotted garden compost should help with the problem in the long term, and also heavy dressings of bulky organic matter when winter digging will gradually eliminate it. On very acid soils, an application of lime is helpful. Alternatively, if such manures are not available, Dolomite or magnesium lime-stone can be applied in winter to acid soils, at the rate of 210 g per sq m (7 oz per sq yd).

Manganese deficiency: the disease called 'speckled yellows' which also appears on spinach, is really a symptom of manganese deficiency. Affected plants have leaves with yellow blotches between the veins, and the leaves tend to curl up, usually in mid-summer. Both very sandy and very alkaline soils can be deficient in manganese. Some natural recovery can occur; the long varieties seem much less susceptible. In severe cases, apply a foliar spray of manganese sulphate at the rate of 60 g in 22. 5 L of water (2 oz in 5 gal of water) with a few drops of liquid detergent.

Varieties

Long

Cheltenham Green-top: long, tapered shape and good flesh colour; very good variety for sandy soils; excellent for clamping for winter use, or lifting from soil as needed.

Cook's Delight: grows 30 cm (1') long and 5 cm (2") in diameter; non-bleeding; good for grating without cooking; no tendency to go woody.

Long Blood Red (Covent Garden): medium sized with small top; excellent for cooking; good in dry years; can be left in sandy soils in warmer areas for digging up as required.

Intermediate

Formanova: deep red, fine-grained flesh; longish oval or cylindrical shape; excellent for cooking.

Round

Detroit: deep red, rich flesh, rough skin; free from rings; fine-grained texture; crops uniform in shape, foliage and texture; suitable for successional sowing and exhibition work.

Detroit New Globe: dark red flesh, fine-grained texture; free from rings; very uniform crops; excellent for kitchen and exhibition work.

Detroit Little Ball: small variety; suitable for successional summer sowings

Detroit

for late autumn and winter use; very quick grower; good for fitting in after a cleared crop.

Boltardy: similar to *Detroit* variety, but can be sown earlier in season due to its resistance to bolting.

Boltardy Mono-seeded: new variety; exactly like *Boltardy* but graded to produce only one plant per seed; eliminates need for thinning.

Ruby Queen: excellent flavour, texture; holds shape well even when crowded.

Globe: dark crimson flesh; good for successional sowings for year round supplies; excellent for kitchen or exhibition work; can be sown mid-summer.

Ruby Queen

Burpees Golden

Early Bunch: deep-red flesh; good round shape; matures in early summer; very bolt-resistant; do not use for maincrop or late sowings.

Avonearly: rich colour, fine texture; very fast grower, maturing in about ten weeks; bolt resistant; can be sown in late winter.

Dwergina: deep-red colour; globe-shaped variety; because it remains small for a long time it is very suitable for bottling and pickling.

Novelty

Burpees Golden: globe-shaped with bright yellow flesh and orange skin; does not bleed like red varieties; leaves can be cooked and served like spinach.

Snowhite: pale white colour; flesh does not bleed; new variety; curled, wavy leaves can be cooked and served like spinach.

Golden Beet: golden flesh; fine flavour; roots best when picked small; good for salads or pickling; tops can be cooked and eaten like spinach.

Sugar beet

Humming Bird: crisp, juicy white flesh; can be eaten raw or cooked as vegetable or used to replace refined sugar in dessert recipes.

Far left: Formanova

Left: Boltardy

Right: Avonearly

Carrots

Daucus carota (fam. *Umbelliferae*)
Herbaceous biennial, grown as an **annual**
Sowing to harvesting time: early or
forced crops are ready for pulling after about 10-12
weeks, maincrops after 14-18 weeks.
Size: up to 23 × 5 cm (9 × 2″) for long-rooted
varieties; up to 12.5 × 6.5 cm (5 × 2½″) for stump-
rooted types.
Yield: 11.5 kg (25 lb) per 10 m (30′) row for
maincrops, slightly less for early crops.

Carrots are one of the easiest vegetable crops to grow, provided the soil has been well prepared. They are rich in calcium, phosphorus and vitamin A, and are a very popular winter standby, when other vegetables are scarce or expensive in the shops. Although usually considered a winter and early spring vegetable, by successive sowings and giving cold frame or cloche protection, you can crop carrots right through the year.

Carrots can be classified in two different ways: by shape or by the time of cropping. Shapes can be basically divided into three different groups, the short kind, which are round or stump-rooted (sometimes called shorthorn varieties), ideal for early or forced crops; the medium length type, more or less sausage-shaped or with a cylindrical tapering root, suitable for both storage and immediate use, and the long rooted, tapering type, which make a good, late maturing crop and are particularly suitable for exhibition. Long carrots can

reach 90 cm (3′) in length, and should really only be attempted if you have near perfect growing conditions; otherwise, it is best to stick to intermediate or early varieties. A good rule of thumb is: the more difficult the growing conditions, the smaller and quicker growing the varieties cultivated should be.

Carrots, like beetroot, are basically cropped in two ways. Early, quick-growing crops are pulled when quite small and either used raw in salads or cooked. These can be grown under glass or in the open. Their taste and texture when young are considered by many to be superior to fully mature carrot crops; they are sweeter and more tender than maincrops. The larger carrots, sown later in the year and pulled for winter storage, tend to be slightly tougher in texture and less flavourful. Recent developments in plant breeding, however, have resulted in vastly improved maincrop varieties, without the pale, stringy, central core which made them so

The fern-like foliage of carrots; the roots are ready when the leaves begin to curl and die.

unpopular in the kitchen. These new varieties are also tastier.

Carrots are herbaceous biennials grown as annuals. Most people think of all carrots as orange, but the wild carrot from which garden types were developed has a white taproot, and on the Continent purple, white and pale yellow varieties of carrots are grown. Because of their high sugar content, carrots are cultivated for sugar production as well as for use as a vegetable, and for distilling alcohol.

Suitable site and soil

Carrots prefer a deep, light, sandy loam. Early crops grow best in full sun, while maincrops appreciate some shading from hot summer sun. Soil conditions are extremely important, because carrots are a root crop, and must penetrate and build up their structure within the soil. Carrots require a deeply dug bed of friable (crumbly) soil about 45 cm (18″) deep, rich in finely divided particles of humus. Gravelly, heavy clay or stony soil is not suitable, because the roots will be unable to penetrate the soil evenly. Very light, sandy soils are only good for small early carrots; maincrop varieties require more substantial soil. Ideally, carrots should be grown on land with a high water table, so the crop never suffers from drought. This does not mean, however, that waterlogged or badly-drained soil is suitable, as carrots

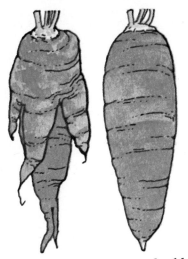

Carrots grown on stony or freshly manured soils may become forked (left), rather than straight.

thoroughly mixed with the soil, so there are no pockets of compost or leafmould. Sandy soils are further improved by the addition of peat; peat helps to bind loose, fast-draining soils and also encourages better drainage and crumb structure on heavy soils that need lightening.

A week to ten days before sowing, rake the bed level and create a fine tilth to ensure maximum germination. After raking, work in 60 g per sq m (2 oz per sq yd) of a general fertilizer which has a low nitrogen content. Rake the fertilizer well into the surface of the bed.

When you have raked the bed level, position a line of string between two stakes across the bed to mark out the row of carrots. Run a corner of a hoe or rake along the line to cut out a V-shaped furrow at least 1.3 cm (½″) deep. Make the rows 15-23 cm (6-9″) apart for early crops, and 30 cm (1′) apart for main-crops.

will not do well in those conditions.

Carrots should be grown on soil which was manured for a previous crop. If manure, garden compost or similar materials are introduced into the soil immediately before growing carrots, some of the crop will tend to be malformed, the roots being split into two or more forks. Large stones can also result in crooked, deformed roots.

On a plot where crops are being grown in a rotation system, carrots should ideally be grown in the previous year's celery bed, or follow lettuce or peas.

Soil preparation
Carrots grow best in sandy loams, but less suitable soils can be adapted for growing carrots by thorough digging and the incorporation of humus-forming manure or garden compost well before the seeds are sown. Ideally, carrots should follow a crop for which the ground was previously manured but, if necessary, major soil preparation can take place early in the autumn before sowing, the soil being left rough over winter. If the soil is very sandy, leafmould or compost will enrich it and increase its moisture retention. Make sure the organic matter is sifted and

Sowing
Maincrops are sown from mid-spring to the end of mid-summer, the later the better, to avoid attacks from carrot fly. Early crops are sown outdoors from the beginning of spring, and at fortnightly or monthly intervals until late summer, to have a continuous supply. There are about 18,000 seeds per 30 g (1 oz), and the seeds will remain viable for five years if properly stored. Pelleted seeds are available and, although more expensive to buy, they are easier to handle and cut down the amount of thinning required.

Carrots prefer warm soil and grow best when not checked by cold. Seeds may fail to germinate if sown during a prolonged cold spell. If the weather is bleak at the time you planned to sow, use cloches of horticultural glass or plastic, or plastic mini-tunnels to warm up the soil in advance and to protect the seedlings. Make sure the end flaps of the tunnels are closed, or conditions will be very windy inside them, and their whole purpose will have been defeated.

There are several methods of sowing carrot seeds. They should be sown as

1. At least a week before sowing, apply a compound fertilizer to the site.

2. Take out narrow drills about 2 cm ($\frac{1}{2}''$) deep, and 15-22 cm (6-9$''$) apart.

3. Sow the seeds in the drill as thinly as possible to avoid overcrowding and lessen thinning later.

4. Cover the seeds and firm the soil, and then level the surface by pulling a rake lightly over the rows.

thinly as possible, to avoid waste and the fiddly task of thinning out. Pelleted seeds can be placed singly in the drills, 2.5 cm (1$''$) apart. A traditional method is to mix the seeds with sand, and then sow the mixture evenly along the drill. You can also mix radish seed with the carrot seed. The radishes will be ready for harvesting early on and this is an easy way of thinning the carrot row. Alternatively, you can sow carrot seed either in pinches between finger and thumb, or by carefully shaking the seed into the drill direct from the packet with the hand held just a few centimetres above the drill. Whatever method of sowing is used, the drill should have been

thoroughly watered the day before sowing, if the soil is at all dry.

After sowing, replace the soil by gently covering the drill, so that the seeds are no more than 0.6 cm ($\frac{1}{4}''$) deep, using the back of a rake. A better but more painstaking method of doing this job is to place your feet on either side of the drill, and shuffle forward along the row, with your toes pointing outwards and your feet pushing soil into the drill. This action safely covers the carrot seed and at the same time gives the row a gentle firming. After covering the seed, rake the soil level by lightly pulling the rake down the row—never across it. Raking across the row would disturb or

17

actually displace some of the seeds. Germination normally occurs from 14-18 days after sowing, but may be a few days longer in cold conditions. If a heavy rain threatens immediately after sowing, cover the drills with mats so the rain does not beat down the soil.

Thinning and general cultivation

The essential task of thinning should begin when the greenery is about 2.5 cm (1″) high. The best time to thin your carrots is after a rain shower; the water loosens the soil and makes the seedlings easier to lift. Doing this work in the evening seems to lessen the chance of attack from carrot fly.

If the carrots were sown in groups, pull out the smallest seedlings in each cluster; if sown continuously along the drill, thin initially to 1.2 cm ($\frac{1}{2}$″) apart. The carrots from the first one or two thinnings will be tiny, but the last thinnings in the early crop can be used in the kitchen. Early crops should have a final distance of 5 cm (2″) between each root; the maincrops should be thinned to a final distance of 10-15 cm (4-6″) apart.

Try not to bruise or break the leaves while thinning, as the pungent odour is very attractive to carrot flies. For the same reason, remove all thinnings immediately and bury them well in the middle of the compost heap. Because firm soil discourages the female fly from laying eggs, water the rows after thinning to firm the soil and fill any holes created by the removal of seedlings. If the soil is cracking because of dry weather, it needs water for the same reason, as well as to supply the carrots. Keep weeds under control, and do not allow the crop to run short of water during dry spells.

Frame cultivation

Forcing varieties of carrots can be grown to mature at times when bought carrots are expensive. Sow the seed on a hot-bed in a cold frame in mid-winter if the weather is mild, otherwise wait until the weather warms up in late winter or early spring. Make the hot-bed from a mixture of manure and other humus-containing

Marshall Cavendish/Clay Perry

Young carrot seedlings just after thinning; try not to damage the leaves while thinning.

1. Hoe regularly between the rows of seedlings to remove weeds.

2. When the seedlings are 2.5 cm (1″) high, thin to a spacing of 1.2 cm (½″) apart. Water the soil before thinning.

3. Firm in the remaining plants and water the ground to deter the carrot fly, which is attracted by the carrot smell.

4. Sprinkle general fertilizer between the plants in the rows, and water the ground again.

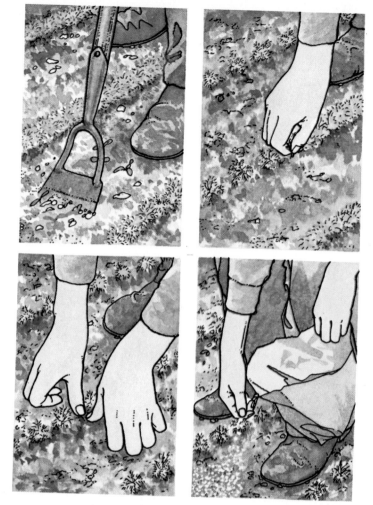

materials that create their own heat by fermentation. The hot-bed for out-of-season carrots should be a gentle one, consisting of a basic layer of straw and rotted manure mixed with rotted leaves. Stack up this mixture until it is about 15 cm (6″) deep. Turn it over and moisten it every day for about a week to encourage fermentation, then flatten it and cover it with about 15 cm (6″) of good garden loam.

Scatter seeds of a stump-rooted carrot variety thinly over the soil, work them in just below the surface with a hand fork, and firm the bed with a wooden board. Water frequently, give ventilation if the weather allows, and cover the frame with sacking or other protection on frosty nights. Do not allow the temperature to fall below 7°C (45°F). Thin first to about 2.5 cm (1″) apart, then to 5 cm (2″); these second thinnings should be big enough to use in the kitchen. When grown in a cold frame, carrots can be sown with lettuce or radishes; these can be harvested fairly quickly, giving the long term carrot crop room to grow.

Carrots can also be forced in unheated cold frames or cloches out of doors, from late winter onwards. Cultivation is the same as for carrots grown on a hot bed. Without the additional warmth of a hot bed, though, the carrots will take longer to mature.

1. Water the ground the night before harvesting so that the young carrots can be easily pulled by hand.

2. To lift mature carrots in autumn, a fork is necessary.

3. Before storing, use a sharp knife to cut off the tops close to the neck.

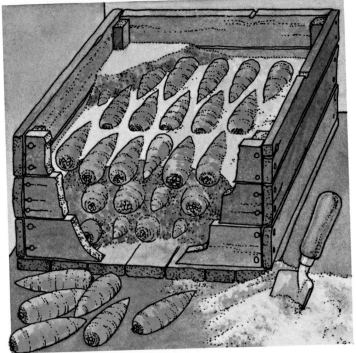

4. Autumn crops can be stored for winter use. Pack them evenly between layers of dry sand in a large wooden box, and keep the box in a frostproof shed.

Harvesting and storing

Once they have reached the desired size, short-rooted early varieties can be harvested from early summer, and harvesting can continue for several weeks. These carrots are at their best and most tender when still quite small, between 2.5 and 5 cm (1-2″) long. Earlier thinnings can also be used, although because of their small size they are a bit awkward to deal with in the kitchen. If the ground is dry, water thoroughly the night before pulling, so the carrots come out of the soil without being damaged.

Although carrots are reasonably frost-hardy, it is a good idea to lift maincrop carrots by the end of mid-autumn. If you live in a particularly mild area, you can leave them in the ground well into winter, but cover the crop with bracken or clean dry straw whenever heavy frost threatens. If left in the ground all winter, though, they are vulnerable to attack by frost, carrot fly and slugs.

When carrots are fully mature and ready for lifting, the outer leaves begin to wilt and the remaining foliage curls up. This is an indication that they have stopped growing, and there is no point in leaving them in the ground any longer.

Choose a dry day at the end of the season to lift the crop. Use a garden fork to loosen the carrots from the soil, and then pull them out by the foliage. After lifting, cut off the foliage near the crown and put it on the compost heap. Remove all the soil adhering to the roots and examine the carrots carefully before storing. Any which have been accidentally speared by the fork during the lifting operation should be set aside to be eaten at once, as damaged carrots quickly rot.

Carrots can be stored outdoors in a hole filled with dry sand and covered with straw, or in a clamp like potatoes (see chapter on POTATOES for storing in a clamp). If properly constructed, the carrots can be kept in the clamp through winter and well into spring. These storage methods are most useful if you have a very large crop; for moderate or

MAKING A CLAMP

1. Choose undamaged carrots, and pile them on dry ground in a conical heap, thin ends pointing inwards.

2. Cover over the carrots with a layer of clean, dry straw at least 15 cm (6″) thick all around.

3. Cover over the straw with a 15 cm (6″) layer of soil. Leave a ventilation hole at the top.

small-sized harvests, it is more convenient to store them indoors in a box in a cool frost-proof shed or cellar. To do this, fill a box with a 5 cm (2″) layer of sand, and then place a layer of carrots head to tail, on the sand, followed by alternating layers of sand and carrots. The final layer should be sand, and the carrots can be easily removed from the box as needed.

Carrots stored in a clamp will keep firm and fresh for several months; carrots stored in boxes will keep for a slightly shorter period of time.

Exhibition tips

The type of carrot you exhibit depends to a large extent on the show date. For early shows, in mid to late spring, select quick-maturing varieties. These do best when sown on a hot bed in a cold frame in mid-winter. Fresh manure or partially-rotted garden compost, to which an activator has been added, will provide the heat necessary to get the carrots growing. The fermenting material should be covered with 15 cm (6″) of fine sifted soil.

For early or mid-summer shows, you can sow one of the larger varieties of carrots in late winter or early spring. If the weather is not unseasonably cold, a hot bed will not be necessary, although cold frame protection is still beneficial. Make sure the soil is absolutely first class, sandy loam; otherwise, prepare boreholes with a crowbar 45 cm (18″) deep and 30 cm (1′) apart in all directions. These boreholes should be filled with sifted old hot bed soil or fine topsoil mixed with sand. You can also show short quick-growing carrots at mid-summer exhibitions.

As long as you have thinned them to 10 cm (4″) apart in the early stages of growth, you should be able to select good specimens from your garden without any additional work being needed.

For late summer shows, sow in mid-spring and again in late spring, in the open ground. If your soil is badly drained, and you are still determined to produce prize-winning carrots, grow them above ground in large clay drain-pipes filled with good sandy compost. Barrels are also suitable. Remember, though, that containerized soil dries out much more quickly than ground soil. The water supply must be consistant; if the soil dries out and then is thoroughly drenched, the roots will split.

Carrots grown for late shows benefit from a bit of shade, perhaps given by neighbouring plants; shaded soil tends to conserve moisture. Carrots, particularly those grown in boreholes, sometimes grow up out of the ground, and the exposed shoulders then turn green or become otherwise disfigured. As soon as you see them beginning to push out of the ground, gently draw soil up around the carrots to cover them, and repeat as necessary. Leave the carrots in the ground until as near as possible to the show date. The one exception is if prolonged rain threatens. To avoid having the carrots split from excess water, lift and store them in moist sand until the show.

Although you can pull carrots out of the ground by their leaves, the skin will be marred in the process. Dark vertical scratches will appear from the friction between the carrot and soil particles. If the ground is soft, it may be all right to pull out the quick-growing, small varieties, but the intermediate and long varieties should be dug out with a spade. Dig carefully until you have completely exposed one side of the carrot, from the surface of the soil down to the tip of the root, and gently lever it out.

Have plenty of wet sacking nearby to wrap around the newly dug carrots; they should never be allowed to dry out. Wash them fairly quickly at this stage with cold water and a sponge; carrots which have split or otherwise damaged roots will then be exposed and can be discarded for show use, although they will probably be perfectly all right for cooking. At this stage reject any carrots which are pale or weak in colour and those which have green or otherwise

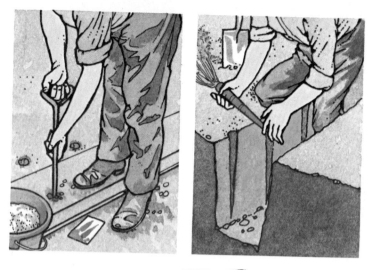

1. To grow long carrots for show, use a crowbar to make holes 45 cm (18″) deep for sowing.

2. Harvest the carrots carefully by digging a trench alongside the row. Lift the roots gently.

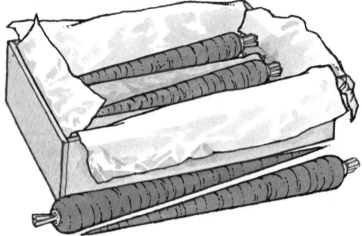

3. Pack long carrots for transporting to the show by placing them tightly, head to toe, in a tissue paper lined box. The carrots must be dry, and the tops cut back to 2.5 cm (1″).

disfigured shoulders. Asymmetrical or bulgy carrots should also be rejected for the show bench. After this preliminary selection has been made, cut off the fine, fibrous roots as close as possible to the main roots with a sharp knife.

If you are packing the carrots to take to the show, remember that much damage can be done if the roots are packed too loosely and can roll against each other in the packing box. Give the carrots a final wash, again with water and a sponge. Never scrub the carrots or you will damage the skin, and never oil them. They should be packed dry and wrapped tightly in tissue paper, with the foliage cut back to 2.5 cm (1″) from the carrot

top. Then wedge the roots tightly into the box, the widest part of one carrot adjacent to the narrow root of the next.

Although it may vary from show to show, the carrots are usually divided into two categories: long pointed varieties, and all other types. Six is the usual number required for single displays, and ten for collections of vegetables. Carrots look best when displayed in pyramids on a plate and garnished with parsley. To keep the carrots fresh until judging, spray them with a fine mist of water. The judges will look for well-shaped carrots, as uniform as possible, with clear, bright colour. The texture should be firm, and the flesh tender and juicy.

Varieties

Early

Nantes-Champion Scarlet Horn: cylindrical roots, free from fleshy core; flesh dark red; 10-12 cm (4-5″) long; good for growing under cloches and successional sowings.

Amsterdam Forcing: very popular stump-rooted carrot, earliest to mature; excellent for successional sowings or growing under cloches.

Parisian Rondo: almost completely round roots 5 cm (2″) in diameter when fully grown; useful for forcing or sowing in succession.

Early Nantes: small, cylindrical, blunt-ended carrot; suitable for forcing and eating raw.

Nantes-Tip Top: cylindrical, stump-ended roots 15 cm (6″) long; flesh coreless and sweet; good for maincrop harvesting as well as early crops.

Little Finger: slender, quick-growing carrot of good flavour; useful for early sowing under glass.

Planet: roots round, 5 cm (2″) in diameter; quick-growing, excellent for shallow soils; novelty variety, but crunchy and sweet-tasting.

Pioneer (F$_1$ hybrid): *Nantes* type; quick grower with heavy, uniform crops; cylindrical roots medium-sized, tender

Early Nantes

and sweet.

French Horn Forcing: round variety; very fast growing.

Chantenay Red-cored (Early Market): very fast grower; crops heavy and uniform; stump-rooted.

Short 'n' Sweet: 7.5-10 cm (3-4″) long, excellent flavour; crops well in light or heavy soil.

Konfrix: round, fast-growing and early carrot; suitable for forcing under glass; very tolerant of soil conditions.

Saber (F$_1$ hybrid): new variety; very fast-growing carrot, uniform and vigorous; tapered shape.

Parisian Rondo

Nantes-Tip Top

Brian Furner

Chantenay Red-cored

Brian Furner

Frubund

Sucram: Nantes type variety with high sugar content and very sweet flavour; very small, tapered.

Early Horn: very quick-growing variety; stump-rooted with very little core; suitable for successional sowings.

Frubund: new variety, extremely hardy and early; stump-rooted, and excellent for successional sowing through autumn.

Maincrop

Autumn King-Early Giant: long, blunt-tipped, extra hardy; larger than *Nantes* type, good for storing for winter use;

somewhat resistant to drought and carrot fly.

New Red Intermediate: longest carrot, with bright red colour and good texture; good for winter storing and exhibition work.

Chantenay Red-Cored-Concord: large, stump-rooted medium-early strain; suitable for early, as well as maincrop sowings; can be stored for winter use; good flavour.

Chantenay Red-Cored-Favourite: very popular stump-rooted maincrop variety; good for exhibition work in 'short' class.

Royal Chantenay: stump-rooted variety;

St Valery

Brian Furner

Autumn King—Early Giant

Juwarot

deep red flesh with very little core.

Scarla: stump-rooted, cylindrical roots; first-class flesh colour; excellent maincrop variety.

Scarlet Perfection: long, stump-rooted variety; first-class flesh; keeps well for winter use.

St Valery: good cropper; long, tapering roots suitable for exhibition work.

Autumn King-Vita Longa: long, large carrot with stump-ended roots giving heavy yields; first-class flavour; good for winter storage.

Flakkee: Dutch variety with large, stump-rooted crops; suitable for winter storage and very good for exhibition.

Long Red Surrey: large, tapered maincrop variety suitable for growing on sandy soils.

James Scarlet Intermediate: large, tapered carrot with heavy, uniform crops; good flavour.

Juwarot: cylindrical-shaped carrot; very good flavour and high vitamin A content; very attractive bright orangy-red colour; stores for a long time.

Zino: new variety; very large, cylindrical carrot; excellent for exhibition work and kitchen.

Pride of Denmark: one of the earlier croppers of maincrop varieties; long, tapering roots; bright orange with red cores; fine flavour.

Pests & Diseases

Carrots are largely pest and disease free; most of the problems occur when carrots are improperly stored in autumn and winter. Conscientious storage preparation is the best precaution against most of the diseases listed below. If there is an outbreak, remove and destroy infected carrots immediately, to avoid spreading the disease.

Carrot fly: this very serious pest attacks other vegetables besides carrots; parsnips and celery are also vulnerable. The worst damage is most likely to occur in hot, dry weather, on very free-draining soil. Large crops of carrots, such as those grown on a commercial scale, seem somewhat more susceptible than the average size crop in a private garden or allotment. The carrot fly, which is about 1 cm ($\frac{1}{2}$") long, black with yellow legs and transparent wings, is attracted by the pungent smell of the carrot foliage, and finds small areas of disturbed soil near the rows ideal places to lay its eggs. The tiny pale yellow maggots that emerge from the eggs then burrow into the roots and may devastate the crop. Wilting, reddened foliage is usually the chief symptom above ground; seedlings will be killed.

The main carrot fly attack occurs in

Damage to the roots caused by the maggots of the carrot fly; spring sowings suffer most.

late spring, so by delaying sowing until the end of early summer it is possible to miss it altogether. The second generation of adult flies does not start laying eggs until late summer, and the maggots hatching from these are unlikely to cause serious damage.

Since thinning the young plants unavoidably releases the smell of the foliage, sow the seeds as thinly as possible to reduce the possibility of attack. Do this in the evening, when the fly is less likely to be about, and destroy the thinnings. Never use a hoe to thin out the young crops; disturbing the soil encourages the flies to lay eggs nearby.

Some veteran gardeners sow rows of parsley between the carrots, because the scent of parsley is said to counteract that of the carrot leaves and so distract or deter the fly. Rows of onions between carrot rows are said to have the same beneficial effect. Alternatively, a rag soaked in parrafin oil can be pulled along the rows occasionally to introduce a camouflage scent. You can also use bromophos dust according to manufacturer's directions.

Wireworm: this pest is most serious in gardens which have been newly turned over from grassland, and is unlikely to cause any trouble on land which has been under cultivation for

Carrots with the characteristic symptoms of the fungal disease violet root rot.

some time. The larvae of the click beetle are also damaging on weedy, neglected gardens. The larvae, which are about 2.5 cm (1″) long, shiny and golden-yellow with six legs, live in the soil and eat the roots of many plants besides carrots, severely damaging or killing them.

The best precaution against wireworm is to make sure your ground is cultivated well and often. Hand weed between plants to keep weeds down, and also expose wireworms to insectivorous birds. Seeds treated with insecticide are somewhat less vulnerable. If the soil is badly infested, you can apply insecticides, such as diazinon or bromophos, according to manufacturer's instructions.

Aphids: these weaken the carrots by sucking sap from the foliage, and some forms damage the roots, so are doubly damaging. The foliage of carrots will be stunted, wilted, and greyish-green. To control aphids, apply derris or bioresmethrin as soon as the infestation occurs, and again as necessary. Since they attack during dry weather, keeping the plants well watered will help to ward off and minimize the damage.

Eelworm: there are various sorts of eelworm which attack both herbaceous and vegetable crops. The microscopic, transparent worms live inside the root tissue of the carrot and multiply rapidly, eventually killing the host plant. Eelworms are difficult for the home gardener to control with chemical insecticides as the soil remains infested for some time after the host plant is removed. Once the carrots are infested, the symptoms of which are wilted foliage and distorted roots, all carrots must be dug out and destroyed immediately. You cannot use the ground for growing carrots for at least seven years and all weeds should be destroyed. This is the only absolutely certain method of getting rid of eelworm; otherwise, new crops may be re-infested.

Violet root rot: this is a serious fungal disease which attacks asparagus, parsnips, beetroot and potatoes as well as

GUIDE TO CARROT TROUBLES

Symptoms	Probable cause
Wilted, reddish foliage; seedlings killed; irregular holes in roots	Carrot fly
Wilted leaves, round holes in roots	Wireworm
Wilted, stunted foliage, distorted roots	Eelworm
Wilted, grey-green foliage, white particles present	Aphids
Webs of reddish-violet strands enmeshing roots	Violet root rot
Roots split, often exposing core	Split root
White woolly fungal growths with black spots	Sclerotina rot
Soft, greyish, smelly flesh	Soft rot
Black patches on shoulders of roots	Black rot

carrots. It is a soil-borne disease, and infected carrots will have webs of reddish-violet strands enmeshing the roots. The above ground symptom of infection is yellowing of foliage. There is no chemical cure for violet root rot; grub up and destroy infested plants. As with eelworm, do not replant the site with carrots for several years.

Split root: this is a physiological disorder, rather than a disease, which is usually caused by a fluctuating water supply. If there is a heavy rainfall after a period of drought, the inner flesh of the carrot expands faster than the toughened skin, causing the skin to fissure. The best precaution against split root is to ensure that the carrots are never allowed to go for long periods of time without water.

Sclerotina rot: this is a problem which occurs under improper damp storage conditions. The symptoms of sclerotina rot are white woolly fungal growths, first seen near the crowns of the roots; in these growths form black resting spore-bodies which can later infect nearby carrots. The best precaution is to ensure that there is proper ventilation in the clamp or box, and that no damaged carrots are ever stored. If there is an attack of sclerotina rot, remove and destroy all infected carrots.

Soft rot: this is a bacterial disease most often encountered in roots damaged during cultivation or by pests; infected carrots become soft, discoloured and unpleasant smelling in the centre, although the outside may look normal. As with sclerotina rot, remove and destroy infected roots so that the bacteria cannot infect healthy carrots. Heavily manured soil, in which carrots are grown in successive years, predisposes them to the disease.

Black rot: a disease found on stored roots, which shows as black sunken patches, usually near the shoulder of the root. As the fungus is carried on the seed, it should always be obtained from reputable seedsmen. No chemical control is known at present, and affected roots should be destroyed, not put on the compost heap, or returned to the soil.

Ministry of Agriculture, Fisheries & Food

White, woolly fungal growths caused by a severe infection of sclerotina rot.

Jerusalem Artichokes

Helianthus tuberosus (fam. Compositae)
Hardy perennial grown as an annual.
Sowing to harvesting time: 9-11 months.
Size: tubers about 10 cm (4″) by 5 cm (2″), plants 1.5-2.5 m (5-8′) tall.
Yield: approximately 1 kg (2 lb) per plant, with 5 plants per 3 m (10′) row.

The Jerusalem artichoke is an ugly vegetable, which is a pity, because otherwise it is something of a gardener's dream. It is extremely hardy, nutritious and easy to grow, as well as being virtually disease and pest free, and an excellent vegetable for the home gardener with little time. Although it will repay good cultivation with a heavier crop, it will also grow quite happily with a large measure of neglect.

The tubers may be ugly but the plants themselves are quite attractive and will grow to become a feature of your garden. The plant is closely related to the sunflower, *Helianthus annus,* and grows, sunflower-like, to a height of 2.4 m (8′) and more, although it is usual to cut off the tops at 1.5 m (5′) so that there is less likelihood of wind damage. Cutting off the tops also prevents plants from producing flowers, but in temperate regions they rarely do so in any case. Only after exceptionally hot summers will they form their large, yellow, sunflower-like flowers in early autumn, and even then they will not set seed.

The parts of the plant which are eaten are the underground tubers, which are storage organs similar to potatoes. Unlike potatoes, however, they are not smooth but extremely irregular in shape and are covered with knobbly projections, rather like ginger. They are about 10 cm (4″) long by 5 cm (2″) wide and have yellowy-white or purple skins and a smoky flavour. Instead of containing starch, as potatoes do, they contain the sugar, inulin, which can be eaten safely by diabetics. Most people, therefore, find them extremely digestible although unfortunately some are allergic to them.

The name 'Jerusalem artichoke' is perhaps misleading. Jerusalem artichokes are in no way related to globe artichokes, whose flower heads, rather than tubers, are eaten, although some people state that they are similar in taste. Nor have they anything to do with the Holy Land. 'Jerusalem' may be a corrupt

Jerusalem artichokes grow up to 2.4 m (8′) tall and make an attractive garden feature.

form of the Italian name, girasole (sunflower) or of the Dutch place name, Ter Neusen, where the artichokes were grown in the seventeenth and eighteenth centuries.

But, however they got their name, they are a very worthwhile crop for the gardener. They can be boiled, either with or without their skins, fried, baked or made into Palestine soup. They also make a useful salad vegetable at a time of the year when salads are sparse in the garden and expensive in the shops. Simply dice them raw and dress with a vinaigrette sauce. Alternatively, cook the artichokes and serve them cold, rather like potato salad.

Suitable site and soil

When your Jerusalem artichokes are fully developed they will form a row of plants at least 2.4 m (8′) tall, so plant them to suit the layout of the rest of your garden. This may be alongside a fence or wall, or as a screen to hide an unsightly compost heap or old garden shed. Although they prefer an open, sunny site they grow quite happily in a shaded spot. They also make an excellent windbreak. Plant them on the north side of tomatoes, cucumbers or other tender crops.

Jerusalem artichokes are virtually pest and disease free so you can plant them in the same place year after year without mishap. If you cannot afford to leave a permanent space for them, however, choose their site particularly carefully. It is easy to miss a few of the smaller tubers when clearing the ground at the end of the winter and these will grow up like weeds the next year, so pick a site where it will not matter much if you have the odd plant appearing during the following summer.

The hardy Jerusalem artichoke will do well on indifferent soil— provided it is not waterloged—but a little attention to the soil is repaid with a heavier crop. If you have garden compost to spare, dig it in sometime during the autumn or early winter—a good general rate is one barrowload every 8 sq m (9.5 sq yd). Jerusalem artichokes also like plenty of potash, so dress the soil generously with wood ash a few days before planting. Alternatively, you can use fishmeal at a rate of 100 g per sq m (3 oz per sq yd). Lightly hoe the wood ash or fishmeal into the soil.

Do not give any nitrogenous fertilizer or manure at planting, however, as the result will be a luxurious growth of foliage at the expense of tubers and the whole exercise will have been a waste of valuable time and space.

Jerusalem artichokes are not fussy, but they do not grow so well on very acid soils. A few weeks after digging and adding manure, test your soil with a soil test kit and add lime to achieve a pH of 6.0–6.5.

SOIL PREPARATION

1. Jerusalem artichokes are not fussy as to their soil requirements but dislike very acid soils. Test your soil and if necessary add lime to give a pH of 6.0.

2. Sufficient potash, too, is important to get a good crop. Add wood ash just before planting to remedy any potash deficiency your soil might have.

Planting

Jerusalem artichoke tubers are planted in the same way as potatoes. The best tubers to plant are the least knobbly ones, about the size of a small chicken egg. If you can only obtain larger tubers, however, you can cut them into pieces—each with three 'eyes' or buds—and plant these pieces.

Plant the tubers anytime from late winter to early spring, in holes 15 cm (6") deep and 60 cm (2') apart. Use a trowel or dibber to make the holes. If you are planting more than one row, space the rows 1 m (3') apart.

Shoots should start to appear above the ground within two to four weeks, given reasonable weather.

Care and cultivation

Jerusalem artichokes require very little attention but they will need to be weeded during the spring until the plants have grown large enough to shade the soil. Weed, using a hoe, and when the plants reach about 30 cm (1') tall, draw the soil up around the stems of the plants while weeding. In this way you will build up a mound around the stems similar to that used for potatoes. The mound encourages the production of tubers by increasing the amount of buried stem from which the tubers grow and it will also help you when you come to harvesting, as tubers in mounds are easier to lift than tubers buried deep in the ground.

PLANTING
AND
CULTIVATION

1. If you have no small tubers for planting, save on tubers by cutting large ones into small pieces. Each piece should have three buds.

2. Make holes 15 cm (6") deep and 60 cm (2') apart.

3. Plant one small tuber or a piece of a larger tuber in each hole and cover over with soil. Shoots should start to appear above the ground within two to four weeks.

In temperate regions the plants will usually not need to be watered except in very dry years. If the soil becomes dry, however, give plenty of water.

Some gardeners retain moisture in the soil, and also keep down weeds, by mulching round the plants with peat or garden compost once they are about 30 cm (1′) tall. If you do this there is no need to weed or earth up—the mulch itself buries the stems to some extent.

Supporting against the wind

Although Jerusalem artichokes make excellent windbreaks, on exposed sites you run the risk of them being blown down by the occasional gale. Not only would you lose your Jerusalem artichoke crop, but neighbouring vegetables could be ruined at the same time. In a very sheltered spot, alongside a wall for example, you will probably be safe just leaving the plants and giving them no support at all, but elsewhere the plants should be supported with wires. During the summer, hammer a 1.5 m (5′) stake into the ground at either end of each row and at 1.5 m (5′) intervals along long rows. Then join up the stakes with wire at 60 and 120 cm (2′ and 4′) intervals from the ground. When the plants are tall enough, tie them to the wires with string.

Cut off the tops of the plants when they reach about 1.5 m (5′) tall. Taller plants are more likely to be blown over.

4. Weed between the plants drawing soil up around the stems in a mound.

5. On exposed sites, tie the plants to wires to protect them from the wind.

5. Cut the tops off the plants when they reach about 1.5 m (5′) tall if not wanted as a screen.

1. When the tops die down in the autumn, cut them off about 30 cm (1') from the ground. Leave the cut stalks to mark the position of the tubers underground.

2. Fork the tubers up, being careful not to spear any or to leave any in the ground. If tubers are left, they will grow up next year like a weed.

3. Store a few tubers, sandwich fashion, in containers of dry peat or sand for winter periods when fresh tubers cannot be lifted from frozen ground.

Harvesting and aftercare

When the leaves and stems begin to turn brown and die back in the late autumn cut them down to about 30 cm (1′) from the ground. Chop the stems up and add them to your compost heap.

You can harvest all the crop as soon as the stems have been cut down in the autumn, but you are better advised to leave the tubers in the ground and to harvest as and when you need them. The tubers can be stored in dry sand or peat, but they taste better eaten fresh from the soil and also have a better texture.

Lift the tubers with a fork in the same way as you would potatoes and add the discarded haulms and roots to your compost heap. Towards the end of late winter, it is best to lift whatever tubers are left in the ground, and use the cleared site to plant new crops in the spring.

Storing the crop

Although Jerusalem artichokes taste best straight from the ground, it is worthwhile lifting some of the crop in the early winter and storing it, so that you have some readily available if the ground freezes hard. To store the tubers, gently rub off any soil adhering to them and place them, sandwich-fashion, in boxes or other containers of dry sand or peat. Keep them in a cool place. All the tubers should be under the surface of the sand or peat as they will deteriorate if exposed to light. Remember to keep some small tubers for planting.

Exhibition tips

Few people bother to show Jerusalem

A fine crop of large, smooth skinned tubers.

artichokes, which is not surprising as the knobbly tubers are hardly an attractive vegetable. Added to this is the disadvantage that Jerusalem artichokes are rarely ready before late autumn and so can only be exhibited at either autumn or winter shows.

If you do intend to exhibit Jerusalem artichokes, try and grow the variety *Fuseau*, which has more regular tubers. Excessively knobbly tubers will be judged harshly and the other variety, New White, has this tendency.

Lift the tubers with care without damaging the skins and then wash them carefully with a sponge as soon as they are lifted. If damp soil dries on the skins they become discoloured. Allow the tubers to dry.

Once the tubers have dried, select large, less knobbly ones of similar size and colour. The normal number to exhibit is twelve. Select a few more than this to give you a choice at your final selection and immediately store the selected tubers for the show.

Even if the show is a local one they should be stored carefully, as they rapidly deteriorate if exposed to the light and air. Wrap the tubers individually in tissue paper and then again in brown paper or black polythene to exclude the light. Then place them in a box in a cool place until the show.

There is nothing you can do to make Jerusalem artichokes pretty but they can be made to look more attractive with a minimum of effort. Place the tubers in a symmetrical pyramid on a black plate or in a basket.

Varieties

The most likely problem with growing Jerusalem artichokes could well be finding some tubers to plant in the first place. Often the easiest way is to plant tubers bought from your greengrocer; as Jerusalem artichokes are virtually disease-free, you do not run the risk of planting diseased tubers, as you would do if you planted potatoes obtained in the same way. Avoid the old purple varieties, however, as these are usually of poor flavour, and after the first year save your own tubers for replanting.

If you do buy tubers from a seedsman you are very unlikely to be offered any choice. There are only two varieties in general cultivation.

New White: the commonest variety; better flavoured than old purple varieties but with rather knobbly tubers.

Fuseau: a French variety: very worthwhile if you can find it but it is very difficult to find a supplier in England; long smooth tubers with a fine flavour; purple-skinned, but does not produce heavy crops.

Brian Furner

New White

Fuseau

Pests & Diseases

You will be very unlucky if you have serious problems with Jerusalem artichokes. They are extremely hardy and pest and disease free. In most years you should be able simply to forget them until you come to dig them up. Two pests and one disease might just give you trouble, however.

Slugs: large holes eaten into the tubers are usually the work of slugs. These pests are most active in wet summers and on wet and heavy land. A well-kept garden discourages them by reducing the number of places where they can hide. You can trap slugs in piles of rotting vegetable matter which you should inspect daily, destroying any slugs you find. Alternatively, if their attacks are severe enough to warrant it, use a proprietary slug bait according to the manufacturer's instructions.

Swift moth: swift moths are another soil-borne pest which may also eat holes in the tubers. The dirty white caterpillars which are the larvae of the moths, live in the soil and feed on the roots of Jerusalem artichokes and other plants, particularly weeds. A well-kept garden with few weeds is less likely to become infected. If you do suffer from swift moths, however, try lightly forking the soil to bring the caterpillars onto the soil surface where they are eaten by insect-catching birds. If the attack is severe you can also spray the soil with trichlorphon.

Sclerotina rot: this disease appears as a white, fluffy fungus which eventually produces black resting spores. The disease is worst in cold damp conditions. Stored roots are particularly susceptible but occasionally the stems at ground level and tubers of growing plants are also attacked. Pull up and destroy all infected plants and do not store any damaged roots, as the rot will quickly spread to the healthy tubers.

GUIDE TO JERUSALEM ARTICHOKE TROUBLES

Symptoms	Probable cause
Large holes eaten in tubers	Slugs
Smaller holes in tubers, occasionally with dirty white caterpillars inside them	Swift moth caterpillar
White fluffy fungal growth with black spots	Sclerotina rot

Swift moth larvae eat holes in the tubers.

Sclerotina attacks both the stems and tubers.

Ministry of Agriculture/Fisheries & Food

Onions

Allium cepa (fam. *Alliaceae*)
Hardy biennial cultivated as an **annual.**
Sowing to Harvesting Time: 14-23 weeks for bulb onions; 6-9 weeks for spring onions; 12 weeks for pickling onions; 18 weeks for shallots.
Size: average bulb diameter 5-10 cm (2-4″), although much larger ones can be grown; plants grow to 50 cm (20″) high; spring onions about 1 cm (⅓″) or less in diameter and 15–30 cm (6–12″) high; shallot bulbs 2–5 cm (¾–2″) diameter, plants grow to 30 cm (12″) high.
Yield: bulb onions 20 bulbs, each about 120 g (4 oz) per 3 m (10′) row; shallots 15 plants, each bearing about 240 g (8 oz) of bulbs per 3 m (10′) row; spring onions about 60 onions per 90 cm (3′) row.

Onions are among the most regularly used of all vegetables, and they are well worth growing at home. Unlike many crops there is little possibility of waste— most onions store so well that whatever you grow you can eventually use up. Another major advantage for many home growers is that an onion crop can be grown on the same site for years, but it can also fit well into a crop rotation, providing a break from brassicas, peas, beans or potatoes.

Onions do best in an open sunny site. The onion grower is rather at the mercy of the weather, in that a period of drought when the bulbs are forming can result in a very disappointing crop. If you can keep watering regularly during a drought this is fine. But if the bulbs reach a point when they get really dry and growth stops, then a sudden drenching can be disastrous, causing distorted growth, split bulbs and thick 'necks'. So, one of the key points to remember is to pull the crop as soon as possible once growth has stopped.

Main types of large onions
The original species of onion has split into several types; the main kinds of interest to the gardener are:
A spring-sown maincrop, harvested in autumn.
Onion 'sets', small bulbs planted in spring for quick growth.
Japanese varieties, a new range of onions, sown in late summer to continue growing over a mild winter and produce a crop the following midsummer.
An autumn-sown crop, harvested as bulbs in the following autumn.

Preparing the soil
Onions need a firm, loamy soil, although good crops can be obtained on any

1. After manuring in autumn, work in 30 g per sq m [1 oz per sq yd] of a compound fertilizer before sowing.

2. Immediately before sowing, rake the seed-bed to a very fine tilth; make the surface as level as possible.

3. Tread down the soil to firm it, but not when it is sticky. Heavy soil needs only a very light firming.

4. Draw drills 1.5 cm [½″] deep and 30-45 cm [1-1½′] apart. Sow seed quite thickly, then barely cover and firm.

5. Sowings under cloches may be made up to 8 weeks earlier than those in the open; warm soil with cloches first.

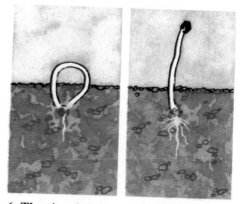

6. The tip of the onion seedling feeds from the seed at first. Do not disturb it; it will soon straighten (right).

7. To control onion fly, apply bands of diazinon granules between drills; do not thin if the soil is dry.

8. Thin the young plants in two stages to a final distance of 15 cm [6″] apart; use thinnings for salads.

9. Water regularly during the growing season to avoid any check in growth, which can produce inferior bulbs.

10. Weed regularly by hand close to plants to avoid loosening soil around roots; elsewhere hoe carefully.

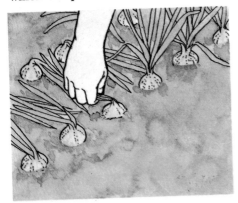

11. In late summer, when leaves are yellow and dying, bend them over to expose bulbs to light and air.

12. Harvest by lifting bulbs carefully with a fork; remember that Japanese varieties must be used immediately.

suitably prepared ground. The land must be well drained. Onions prefer a light soil to a heavy one, and it is a good idea to correct any acidity to about pH6 by applications of lime at a rate based on the result of a soil test.

For the best results, dig an organic plant food (farmyard manure or a good quality garden compost) into the soil several months before sowing (eg in autumn for beds where you will be sowing in spring). A barrow-load of manure or compost for every 7 sq m (9 sq yd) should be sufficient. A compound fertilizer may also be applied just before sowing at the rate of 30 g per sq m (1 oz per sq yd) and worked well into the soil. All types of onion need a firm, compact seed-bed of fine soil. Rake the ground before sowing and tread well to firm it.

Sowing

The spring-sown maincrop: Sow outdoors as early in spring as soil conditions will permit. The soil should be moist but not wet; if soil does not stick to your boots but still feels damp then it is ready for sowing. Sow the seed in drills 1.5 cm ($\frac{1}{2}''$) deep and 30-45 cm (1-1$\frac{1}{2}'$) apart, and sow fairly thickly—about 10-20 seeds per 30 cm (1′) row—because the thinnings can be used as salad onions. The period from sowing to germination, on average, is 14-21 days. Thin the young plants in two stages, the first to about 5 cm (2″) apart, and then to about 15 cm (6″) apart.

As with most vegetables, an advantage can be gained in spring by sowing under cloches. These sowings can be made up to eight weeks earlier than those in the open. The extra weeks are particularly useful with onions, as the plants need a long growing period, so that bulbs sown under cloches tend to be larger. Remove cloches when all danger of frost is past.

You can also get a head start by sowing in late winter in a cold frame. Sow as you would for growing under cloches, and harden off for planting out in mid-spring.

Onions sown under cloches or in frames have two other advantages over later-sown crops. In the first place, they

GROWING ONIONS FROM SETS

1. Before planting onion sets, cut off old leaves that would attract the birds after planting.

2. By mid-spring, plant sets 15 cm [6″] apart in shallow drills 30 cm [1′] apart, with 'necks' uppermost.

3. Have a look at the sets a week or two after planting; press back into the soil any that have moved.

A fine crop of onions, with their tops bent over to hasten ripening.

grow quickly and make much of their growth while the soil is still moist from the winter rains, thus avoiding a severe check at a critical stage during a summer drought. They are also sufficiently well grown to resist the attacks of the onion fly, which is active in late spring and summer.

Growing onions from sets: Many gardeners achieve a flying start by planting onion 'sets'. These are small onion bulbs which have had their growth arrested in the previous autumn. In the past, gardeners avoided onion sets because they tended to bolt and run to seed. Nowadays, however, sets are carefully treated and stored, and they are often easier to grow and keep than varieties raised from seed, particularly in areas where the summers are cool and wet. Buy only certified sets from a reputable seed merchant.

Onion sets are imported from Europe or sub-tropical zones for planting in temperate climates in mid-spring. Plant them in rows 30 cm (1') apart with the bulbs 15 cm (6") apart in each row. Set them in the soil with the 'neck' at the top just visible above the surface.

Like onions sown under cloches, onions grown from sets enjoy the advantage of making much of their growth while the soil is still moist and of being sufficiently well grown to resist onion fly attacks.

Japanese varieties: Sow in late summer, following the instructions for the maincrop but sowing slightly more thickly. When grown successfully, these varieties should fill the gap between using the last stored onions from the previous year's spring sowing and the availability of the new crop next autumn. So far, Japanese onions have not been fully tested in all climatic zones, although they are widely available in the UK and have proved successful in most areas.

Autumn sowing: Sowing onions in autumn outdoors gives the same results as sowing in spring under cloches or planting onion sets. The bulbs from autumn sowings should be ready for harvesting a month or so earlier than those from a spring sowing. But autumn sowings are worthwhile only if your garden is fairly warm, and the site chosen should be quite sheltered.

The seed should be sown in early autumn to give the plants enough time to attain a reasonable size—about 15 cm (6″) in height—before the onset of winter frosts. Sow as you would for the spring maincrop, but a bit more thickly to allow for casualties. Onions are hardy but not completely so, and a severe winter will cause damage. It is important to select the correct varieties, bred for autumn sowing. Onion plants bought from nurserymen for transplanting in spring should also be of the autumn varieties.

Care during growth

Because onions produce tall, thin, hollow leaves, they are particularly susceptible to weed competition. Hoe the soil frequently but shallowly to avoid loosening the compact soil around the onion roots or damaging the bulbs. Hand-weeding, which does not damage the roots, will almost certainly be necessary. A sedge peat mulch will help to control the weeds, but it should not cover the tops of the bulbs.

Onions should be watered well and regularly throughout the growing season to avoid any check in growth, which can result in bulges in the bulbs, in thick necks and thin bulbs, or in splitting.

Examine onion sets a week or two after planting, as they tend to rise out of the soil and may 'travel' several centimetres from the place where they were planted. If this has happened, press the sets back into the soil. They may also be pulled out of the ground by birds.

During the growing period onions

RIPENING AND STORING ONIONS

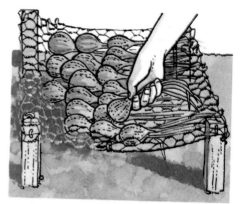

1. If the ground is wet at harvesting time, ripen bulbs by placing them on a platform raised from the ground.

2. If it is raining at harvesting time, ripen bulbs in a cold frame, as shown here, or move them into a shed.

3. You can store ripe, thoroughly dry bulbs in trays with slatted bases in an airy, dry, frost-proof place.

STORING ONIONS ON A STRING

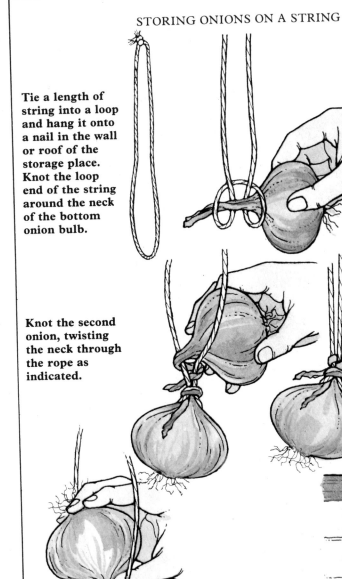

Tie a length of string into a loop and hang it onto a nail in the wall or roof of the storage place. Knot the loop end of the string around the neck of the bottom onion bulb.

Knot the second onion, twisting the neck through the rope as indicated.

Add the rest of the bulbs one by one, to form a spiral 'rope' of onions.

need a lot of nourishment. Feed the plants with either liquid manure at regular intervals until mid-summer, or hoed-in applications of a nitrogenous fertilizer, such as nitrate of soda, at the rate of about 30 g per 3 m (1 oz per 3 yd) in late spring or early summer.

When the bulbs are ripening, as indicated by the yellowing and dying back of the leaves, discontinue any watering or feeding. In dry weather the leaves will bend over naturally but, if the summer is wet and this has not happened, bend over the tops to expose the neck of each bulb to the sun, to hasten the ripening process. It may take five weeks for large bulbs to ripen.

Harvesting the crop

Bulb onions will be ready for harvesting throughout the summer and autumn, according to the time of sowing. The earliest are the new Japanese varieties which should mature around mid-summer. Japanese onions are for immediate use; most other varieties can be used at once or can be stored. Very large onions do not store as well or as long as smaller bulbs, so use the large ones first.

A dry day is best for harvesting onions. Lift them gently with a fork or pull them by hand and, in dry weather, lie the

Onions can be hung on a wall outdoors if the weather is warm and dry, but take them indoors at the first sign of dampness or of frost.

bulbs flat on the ground or on sacking. Turn them now and again to ensure even ripening. The onions are ready for storing when they are thoroughly dry with brittle, papery leaves. In a wet season, the drying process will take longer, and you should lift the onions onto a platform raised above the ground, allowing the circulation of air beneath it. A tray of small-mesh wire netting is ideal. This can be moved into a shed if wet weather persists.

Storing the crop

Bulb onions are normally grown for storing and use in autumn and winter. Onions in store will start to produce green shoots and, if allowed to, flower-heads in the following spring, so only keep them for a limited time and check them for signs of decay or growth.

Bulbs for storing should be perfectly healthy and quite dry. Discard any that are not. Probably the best method of storing is the traditional 'string' of onions: tie each bulb to a length of rope suspended from the roof of a shed or outhouse, arranging them spirally around the rope. Alternatively, onions can be stored on trays of wire netting, suspended in rope or nylon nets, or placed on wooden shelves, although it is best to have air circulating all around the bulbs. The shed in which they spend the winter must be dry, airy and frost-proof.

Aftercare

The onion is among the most economical of plants in its production of foliage. By the time the bulb has ripened there is very little left of other parts of the plant. Consign any dead leaves to the compost heap if they are free from pests and disease; otherwise, burn them.

Salad and pickling onions

Salad or spring onions, also known as scallions, can be sown in autumn, spring or summer, for pulling when young and green to be used raw in salads. Small, silver-skinned onions for pickling are sown in spring and harvested in summer.

Spring onions are sown in the same soil and conditions as for the maincrop. Pickling onions prefer a light, thin soil. Make the drills a bit wider than those for the larger varieties, and sow the seed very thickly. Both are very quick-growing, maturing in about 12 weeks.

Exhibition tips

Sow the seed in mid-winter in a greenhouse heated to 13°C (55°F), so that the bulbs will be fully ripe in time for the early autumn shows. Sow the seeds 2.5 cm (1") apart in 7.5 cm (3") deep seed boxes filled to within 2.5 cm (1") of the top. Use a light compost with a small amount of sharp sand added. Cover the seeds with no more than 0.5 cm ($\frac{1}{4}$") of the compost and sand mixture and keep the light out by covering the boxes with glass and newspaper until the seed germinates.

Then remove the paper and prop up the glass. Remove the glass altogether after a few days and place the boxes near the light. Keep the compost quite moist. When the seedlings have four leaves, prick them off individually into 9 cm ($3\frac{1}{2}$") pots and move them to an unheated frame in early spring. If necessary, support the plants with slender canes.

After hardening off, set out the plants into their permanent bed in mid to late spring, spacing them 30 cm (1') apart in rows 30 cm (1') apart. Choose only those plants that have firm, green leaves and white, unbroken roots.

After this, cultivate as normal, although you can give more nitrogenous food (as dilute liquid manure) and a light dressing of potash in mid-summer. Just before you are ready to lift the bulbs remove a little of the soil from around the neck, also any loose outer skin, so that the bulbs get plenty of sun and develop the best possible colour.

A few days before harvesting, loosen the roots by partly lifting the bulbs carefully with a fork. After harvesting, when the necks should be limp, place the bulbs in a slightly shaded part of the greenhouse or a sunny room to ripen.

Varieties

This is a guide to the basic characteristics of some of the most popular varieties of onion. Your local garden centre will probably feature a selection of these which are most likely to suit the climate and soil in your area. Other key points to remember are whether you want a strong or mild flavour, and for how long you will want to store your crop of onions.

Varieties for Spring Sowing
Ailsa Craig: an old favourite, and one of the best; the large, golden-brown bulbs have a mild flavour and are very long-keeping.
Bedfordshire Champion: very reliable heavy cropper; well-flavoured, long-keeping bulbs.
Giant Zittau: produces semi-flat, medium-sized, brown-skinned, long-keeping onions.
Rijnsburger: a group of several hybrids; all reliable heavy croppers producing large, long-keeping bulbs.
Hygro: new variety; produces uniform-sized bulbs with pale skin and white flesh.
White Spanish: very large, flat bulbs; will keep for a very long time.
Mammoth Red: very large, sweet bulbs; red-skinned, good for cooler climates.

Varieties for Autumn Sowing
Ailsa Craig: excellent variety equally suited to autumn and spring sowing.
Solidity: very large flattish bulbs; keeps well; not prone to bolt.
Giant Rocca: two types—brown-skinned and yellow-skinned; flattish globe onions; do not store well, however.
Red Italian: medium-sized, flat, red-skinned onions.
Big Ben: large onions with semi-flat shape; non-bolting; golden skin; keeps well.

Japanese Varieties
Express Yellow: earliest of the Japanese types; flattish bulbs with golden-brown skin can crop in early summer.

Much grown for exhibition, Ailsa Craig *is a very large onion variety with a mild flavour.*

Sutton Seeds Ltd. Torquay

Rijnsburger *varieties are heavy croppers with exceptionally good keeping qualities.*

Brian Furner

47

Harry Smith

White Spanish *can be sown in autumn or spring and produces mild, long-keeping bulbs.*

Pat Brindley

For cooler climates, try Mammoth Red *with its large, sweet-tasting, red-skinned bulbs.*

Sutton Seeds Ltd.

Solidity, *quite bolt-resistant, is good for autumn sowing; it gives solid, flattish bulbs.*

Pat Brindley

Express Yellow, *an F_1 hybrid, is the earliest of the autumn-sown Japanese varieties.*

Kaizuka (Kaizuka Extra Early): for sowing in late summer to crop in mid-summer the following year; straw-coloured, flat onions.

Senshyu: heaviest cropper of Japanese types; for sowing in early autumn; straw-coloured, semi-globe-shaped onions.

Presto: of Swiss origin, but very similar to the Japanese varieties and treated as one; sow in late summer for onions the following mid-summer; semi-globe bulbs with a good flavour.

Onion Sets

Stuttgarter Giant: suitable for all regions, particularly where seeds are difficult to grow; resistant to bolting; very long-keeping.

Sturon Autumn Gold: large, solid onions; long-keeping; does not bolt.

Stuttgarter Giant, *grown from sets, is ideal where onions are difficult to grow from seed.*

A long-established spring onion variety, White Lisbon, *has a good, mild flavour.*

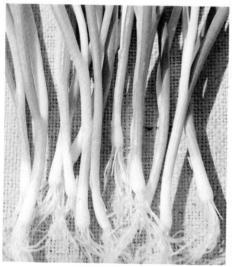

Ishiko Straight Leaf *is a Japanese spring onion that can be sown in spring or autumn.*

The most popular pickling onion, Paris Silver-skin, *grows quickly and ripens early.*

Rijnsburger Wijbo (Giant Fen Globe): one of the best varieties; specially treated to stop bolting; very early globe-shaped onions with golden skins; mild flavour.

Spring Onions
White Lisbon: most common variety for spring onions; quick-growing.
White Lisbon Winter Hardy: variety for sowing in early autumn to give the earliest spring onions; very hardy.
Ishiko Straight Leaf: new type for spring and autumn sowing; leaves straight and green to the tip; winter-hardy.

Pickling Onions
Paris Silver-skin: small, silver-skinned onions; quick-growing; ripens early.
Cocktail: one-inch bulbs which mature rapidly; well-flavoured pickling type.

49

Pests & Diseases

Onion fly: the most troublesome pest is the onion fly, which resembles a small, grey house fly. It lays its eggs in spring and early summer, on the neck of the bulb, on the leaves and in the nearby soil. When the larvae hatch, from late spring onwards, they tunnel into the plant tissues. Control them by scattering diazion granules in late spring.

Older plants can be attacked, but young onions are particularly susceptible and, if onion fly is prevalent, it may be as well to stop pulling young plants for salad. Lift and burn any affected plants as soon as you see the symptoms of yellowing, drooping foliage, and be sure not to leave any maggots in the ground. Take care not to leave thinnings lying around or to damage roots or leaves.

The flies are attracted to freshly manured beds, so be sure to dig in organic matter several weeks before sowing. Very early sowing will ensure that thinning is done before the onion fly is about to attack the plants. Autumn-sown plants are less likely to be attacked.

Eelworm: eelworms are minute parasites which are invisible to the naked eye. Stem and bulb eelworms may affect onions, causing distorted leaves and swollen bases. There is no really effective chemical control, and an attack is normally a sign of neglect of proper

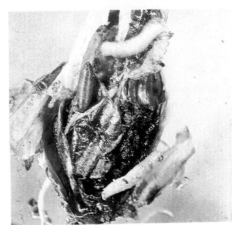

Section of an onion with severe onion fly damage, clearly showing the white larvae.

A Shell Photograph

The effects of eelworm. An infestation is usually due to neglecting crop rotation.

Murphy Chemical Ltd.

crop rotation and a lack of garden hygiene, allowing the pest to build up to dangerous levels. Chickweed can be affected by the same eelworm, so it is important to keep the bed weed-free. Burn any infected plants and make sure that you grow onions in a different place in the garden in the future. After a serious outbreak, it is best to refrain from growing onions in any part of the garden for at least two years. Autumn-sown plants are less liable to be attacked.

White rot: white rot sometimes builds up in crops of salad onions in hot, dry summers. The leaves become yellow and the bases of the bulbs become covered

GUIDE TO ONION TROUBLES	
Symptoms	Probable causes
Yellowing, drooping leaves	Onion fly White rot
Leaves dying back from the tips	Downy mildew
Distorted, misshapen leaves	Eelworm
Black, sooty spots on leaves or bulbs	Smut Smudge
White 'mould' on bulbs	White rot
Bulbs rotting in storage	Soft rot Neck rot

The fungus disease neck rot may affect bulbs in storage. Avoid damp, stuffy conditions.

White rot damage on salad onions, showing fungus on bulb bases and yellowing leaves.

with a white or grey fungus. It can be combated by dusting the soil at sowing time with calomel dust, but the best control is to keep onions away from any affected plot for at least eight years. Plants grown on fertile, organically manured soil are less susceptible to the disease, and some varieties of onions are more resistant than others. The variety White Lisbon, on the other hand, is particularly susceptible to the disease.

Downy mildew Downy mildew, or onion mildew, is a fungus disease which occurs in cool, wet weather. The fungus causes the leaves to die back from the tips and shrivel. Burn diseased plants and do not grow onions on the site for a year, as the disease spores can remain in the soil. Some varieties are more resistant than others.

Neck rot: this seed-borne fungus disease only reveals itself when the onions are in store—by then it is too late. The preventative treatment is to give onion seeds and sets a dusting of benlate before planting. Keep your storage place cool and well ventilated and dry the bulbs thoroughly. Never store damaged onions or those with green fleshy necks.

Soft rot: soft rot, another disease caused by improper storage, causes the bulbs to become glassy and rot into a soft mass. Again, to prevent this follow instructions for proper storage.

Smudge: smudge is a minor fungus disease which is seen as black smudges on the outer scales of the onions. As it does not usually cause major damage, no special treatment is necessary, other than proper harvesting and careful storage.

Smut: smut fungus disease shows as sooty spots and patches on the leaves and bulbs, and it can kill seedlings. Fortunately it is not common in the UK. There is no chemical control; rest the soil as long as possible, destroy the affected plants as soon as you see them, and be extremely careful not to spread the contaminated soil about the garden to ensure against any further attacks. Only young plants are infected.

Grey mould: autumn-sown onions are susceptible to grey mould, which can be recognized by white spots on the leaves. Eventually the leaves die back from the tips. A spraying of captan or colloidel sulphur in early spring can help to prevent this.

Yellow dwarf and shallot virus yellows: yellow dwarf results in stunted stems and yellow-streaked leaves. It occurs mainly in America, but the disease shallot virus yellows is very similar and is found in the UK, although onions are only occasionally affected. Shallot virus yellows is spread by greenfly, so control by spraying with derris or pyrethrum.

Parsnips

Pastinaca sativa (fam. *Umbelliferae*)
Hardy biennial grown as an **annual**
Sowing to harvesting time: 6-11 months
Size: roots up to 45 cm (1½′) long
Yield: about 14 parsnips, each weighing on average 360–450 g
(¾–1 lb), per 3 m (10′) row.

Before the potato was introduced to Europe in the late sixteenth century, its place in European cooking was taken largely by the parsnip. Few vegetables are as easy to grow, as nutritious or as versatile. Parsnips are available as a fresh vegetable throughout the winter, actually improving as the winter progresses and frost gets to the roots. They can be baked, boiled or fried, while some people eat the leaves as a green vegetable, getting double value from their crop.

The problem with growing parsnips is that they have such a long growing season. They are among the first crops to be sown—as soon as the soil is workable in late winter or early spring—and then occupy the land for the rest of the year and are perhaps the last crop to be harvested. They can thus take up land which could be put to more profitable use growing a series of crops.

If you have a small garden you may decide against them for this reason—although you can raise a catch crop, such as radish or lettuce, before the parsnips are established in the spring. But if you have a fair piece of land, and especially if you do not have a lot of time, parsnips are an obvious choice.

Suitable site and soil

Soil is the all-important factor in growing parsnips. Do not bother with them if you have a thin gravelly soil, as you will only get small, mis-shapen roots. The best soil is friable, rich and slightly on the heavy side, although it should not be recently manured as this tends to cause forking, as do stones.

Do not worry if your soil is not the best, however. Almost all well-drained soils will produce a good crop of the shorter varieties although it is worthwhile to try and follow on to land manured for a previous crop. Simply dig the soil about 10 cm (4″) deeper than the length of your intended variety—this will be down to about 50 cm (20″) for the longer varieties—removing large stones. However, if your garden is very stony and removing all the stones is impractical, it may be worthwhile growing in boreholes as you would for exhibition parsnips (see Exhibition tips).

Level the bed off, to give a fine tilth, a day or two before sowing—which will normally be as soon as conditions allow in the late winter or early spring. While you are preparing the bed, rake in a mixture of four parts by volume superphosphate, together with one part each of sulphate of ammonia and sulphate of potash, at the rate of 100 g per square metre ($3\frac{1}{2}$ oz per sq yd).

Parsnips dislike very acid soil and do best in one which is slightly acid, neutral or slightly alkaline, so test the soil with a soil test kit several weeks before preparing the seed bed. If necessary, add lime to achieve a pH of 6.5.

The site you choose for parsnips is not as important as the soil. They prefer an open, sunny site, but they will also grow quite happily in a plot lightly shaded by other plants.

Sowing

The traditional time to sow parsnips is late winter but, unless the winter is mild, the soil is often frozen hard or too wet at this time. In most years you will probably have to wait until early spring before sowing. Although parsnips appreciate a long growing season, you can sow later still, up to late spring if you have to, and still get a worthwhile crop.

Sow the seed in a shallow V-shaped drill about 2 cm ($\frac{3}{4}''$) deep. Take the drill out using the edge of a hoe. If you are sowing more than one row, space the rows 30-45 cm (12-18") apart.

Parsnip seeds are fairly large—a little under a centimetre (about $\frac{1}{4}''$) in diameter—but they are very thin and light. Sow three or four seeds at each station along the drill with about 15-23 cm (6-9") between the stations, depending on the size of your variety. It is a good idea to sow several seeds at each station because, although most of them will germinate, you will then have a good choice when thinning and can ensure that there is a really strong seedling in each position. The seed does not store very well, so always use it fresh.

Because the seed is so light, it is inadvisable to try to sow on a windy day; wait until the weather calms down. One way of making life easier is to use pelleted seed. Several parsnip varieties are available in this form. The pelleted seed is heavier so it will not blow away.

Dig the soil a little deeper than the length of your intended variety, making sure to remove all stones.

Test your soil and if it is very acid, apply lime as necessary to achieve a pH of 6.5.

Work the soil to a fine tilth and prepare drills 30-45 cm (12-18") apart and 2 cm ($\frac{3}{4}''$) deep.

Sow three or four seeds at each station, spacing them 15-23 cm (6-9") apart from each other.

It is a good idea to raise a catch crop of lettuce between the parsnips, to mark your rows.

Thin the seedlings when they are about 5 cm (2") tall, leaving only the strongest at each station.

Water if the weather is dry. This is especially important during the crop's early stages.

Hoe as necessary, taking care not to damage the shoulders of developing roots in any way.

After the seeds have been sown in the drill, cover them with soil (sifted soil is best for this) and firm down. Water if the weather is dry.

Germination takes three to four weeks, and in this time it is quite easy for the row of parsnips to be lost among newly germinated weeds. Weed frequently and carefully. Many gardeners sow a quick-maturing catch crop, such as lettuce or radish, between the stations in the row. This not only gives you an extra crop but also helps to mark the row. If you do not wish to do this, leave your marking line in position until the seeds have germinated.

With correct cultivation, you can achieve a bumper crop like this one, ready for harvesting.

Care and cultivation

Once the parsnips are sown they need very little attention. When the seedlings are about 5 cm (2″) tall, thin all but the strongest at each station. Do not be tempted to use the thinnings; parsnip seedlings do not produce good roots after the check produced by transplanting. Water, particularly during the early stages of the crop, if the weather is dry, and weed frequently. Be very careful when using a hoe to remove weeds that you do not damage the shoulders of the developing roots; you may open the way for attack by canker.

Harvesting

Once the tops of parsnips turn yellow and begin to die back, they are ready for harvesting. Parsnips sown in early spring should be ready in mid-autumn, but do not rush to pull them all up. The flavour of parsnips is improved by frost, which increases the sugar content of the root, so leave most of them in the ground and dig some up when you want them during the winter. Do not leave any in

the ground after February, however, as then they will start to grow again and become woody and useless.

Small parsnips in .light soil can be pulled up once the soil around them has been loosened with a fork. Normally, however, the only way parsnips can be lifted without breaking them is by digging. Begin at the end of the row and dig a hole beyond, but close to, the last parsnip. Dig the hole as deep as the parsnip and loosen the soil around the root, which can be then easily removed without damage. Lift the next parsnip by moving the soil next to it into the hole from which the first parsnip has been taken and continue like this to the end of the row.

You will probably find you have to dig down much further than you expect. The end of a parsnip root tapers off for a considerable length, 15 cm (6″) or more, and has a surprisingly strong grip on the soil. In fact, it will probably be necessary to break off the thinnest part of the root, if you want to avoid digging a sizable hole 45 cm (18″) deep for each root.

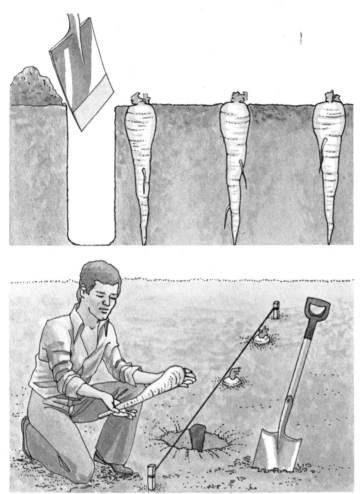

Begin at the end
of the row and
dig a hole close
to the first
parsnip, making
sure it is as deep
as the length you
expect the
parsnip to be.
Loosen the soil
around the
parsnip and you
will then be able
to lift it easily
without damage.
Lift the next
parsnip by
removing the
soil next to it
into the hole you
made for the
first one and
continue like this
down the row.

Although
parsnips are best
left in the
ground, it is a
good idea to
store some for
when frost
makes lifting
impossible.
Store them in
boxes, using
layers of peat or
dry sand.

Once the parsnips have been lifted, cut off any remaining leaves with a knife. The discarded tops are excellent compost heap material.

Storing

Although the best-flavoured parsnips are those lifted and taken into the kitchen straight from the ground, obviously you will not be able to do this when the ground is frozen hard in the middle of winter. To give you parsnips during this period, therefore, you should dig up some roots in the early winter for storing.

Store the parsnips in the same way as you would carrots. Cut any leaves off close to the crowns and then pack the roots in layers of dry sand or peat in a large wooden box. Put a lid on the top to keep out the light and place the box in a cool, dry and airy place.

Exhibition tips

Exhibition parsnips should be long, straight and unforked. Grow a long variety and sow them as early as you can to get the longest possible growing season. Parsnips are unlikely to be ready for an early summer show but should be large enough for late shows.

If you have a first-class, deep, stone-free and friable loam you will probably be able to produce roots sufficiently good for showing by planting them in the normal way, perhaps just spacing them a little further apart, at 30 cm (12″) intervals. If you are not so lucky, however, you will only be able to produce first-class parsnips by sowing in boreholes.

Use a long straight iron rod to make a conical hole about a metre (3′) deep and about 15 cm (6″) in diameter at the top. Drive the rod into the soil and work it in small circular movements to make the hole. Space the holes about 30 cm (1′) apart.

Fill the holes with a good, moist sandy compost which you have first put through a 1.5 cm (½″) sieve. Firm this soil down and then sow in the normal way.

Keep the parsnips well watered throughout the season to prevent cracking, and weed frequently. It is a good idea also to mulch with peat to retain moisture and to keep down weeds.

Harvest the parsnips as late as possible before the show. Be very careful not to damage or scratch them when you dig

EXHIBITION GROWING

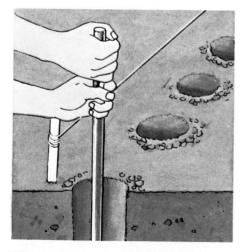

Using a long rod, make holes 30 cm (1′) apart, 1 m (3′) deep and about 15 cm (6″) wide at the top.

Almost fill the holes with sifted soil and sow 3-4 seeds in each. Cover to a depth of 2 cm (¾″).

them up. Use the hole method (see Harvesting).

The normal number of parsnips to exhibit is six in collections and three in single dishes. Pick large, white, straight roots, all of the same size. They should be well-developed with good shoulders and absolutely blemish-free.

After lifting, cut off the tops about 2.5 cm (1″) from the shoulders and shave off all the root hairs with a sharp knife. Then sponge the roots very carefully, and wrap in wet sacking immediately to keep them fresh so that they look their best when you get to the show.

When you get to the show simply lay the parsnips carefully together on the bench in the form of a pyramid, with three roots at the bottom and one at the top. Adjust the roots so that they are close together with as little daylight between them as possible; turn them round so that any bulges on one root fit into a depression in its neighbour. If necessary, tie them together with a piece of soft string, preferably of the same colour as the parsnips. If displayed in a simple manner like this, they will look even better than they are, without appearing over-fussy.

Varieties

The varieties given have been divided into short, medium and long-rooted. Short and medium varieties normally have rounded ends, long-rooted ones taper to a fine pointed tip. If you are exhibiting parsnips or have a good, deep and stone-free soil, choose a long-rooted variety. Otherwise, choose a short or medium variety which is easier to grow on more difficult or shallow soils.

Short-rooted
Avonresister: the shortest variety of all, producing small, conical roots; because it is so small, thin to only 7.5 cm (3″) between plants in the rows; more resistant to canker than most other varieties.

Medium-rooted
White Gem: white smooth skin; some resistance to canker.
Offenham: a broad-shouldered variety particularly suitable for clay or shallow

Avonresister

Before the show, trim back leaf stalks to 2.5 cm (1″) and cut off the rootlets with a sharp knife.

Brian Furner

White Gem

Offenham

Lisbonnais

Hollow Crown

soils; good, sweet flavour; heavy cropper.

The Student: thick tapering roots with excellent flavour; heavy cropper.

Long-rooted

Improved Hollow Crown: long symmetrical root; solid white flesh.

Exhibition Long-rooted: clean, smooth root of fine flavour, a good choice for showing.

Tender and True: clear smooth skin; resistant to canker.

Lisbonnais: very good flavour; a large, well-shaped root; especially good for exhibiting.

Pests & Diseases

Not much is likely to go wrong with your parsnip crop if it is well-grown as part of a crop rotation. Several diseases, such as downy mildew and leaf spot may be unsightly but they do not seriously affect the yield of an otherwise healthy crop. Canker is the worst problem and good cultivation is the best defence against this.

Wireworm: gardens recently recovered from grassland or badly-tended gardens suffer most from this troublesome pest. The shiny yellow larvae, which are about 2.5 cm (1″) long, bore small regular holes in most root crops, including parsnips. Small roots may be almost entirely eaten up.

Keep wireworm down by careful weeding and cultivation. Treat very badly infected land with diazinon or bromophos, and do not plant parsnips or other susceptible crops for four or five years.

Celery fly: although this pest is not as serious on parsnips as it is on celery, it can still do sufficient damage to reduce growth appreciably, because its attacks interfere with the chlorophyll-making mechanism of the leaves. The tiny 0.5 cm (¼″) adult flies lay eggs on the foliage and the small maggots which emerge burrow into and through the leaves, producing white or brownish blisters as they go. Normally, good cultivation will enable the plants to grow back after attack, but in the worst cases the most badly affected leaves should be removed and the remainder sprayed with mal-athion. Alternatively, you can kill the maggots by squeezing them, still in the leaf, between your finger and thumb. If you are particularly troubled by this pest, paraffin-soaked rags hung near the parsnips helps discourage the flies from laying eggs.

Carrot fly: the greenish-black carrot fly lays its eggs in the soil near carrots, parsnips or celery to which it is attracted by the smell of the foliage. The eggs hatch to produce small, pale yellow maggots which invade the roots. These pests are also a problem because the wounds they cause provide a starting point for canker.

Carrot fly is most likely just after thinning because the smell of the damaged foliage of the thinned plants attracts them. Thin in the evening when the flies are less likely to be active, and burn all the thinned plants. Firm the soil around the plants after thinning as this fills in the cracks in the soil and deters the flies from laying eggs. As with celery fly, paraffin-soaked rags help to discourage them. If the problem persists, dust with bromophos according to the manu-facturer's instructions.

Aphids: in a dry summer, greenfly can infest the foliage in large numbers, so that the leaves curl, become yellowish and even cease to grow. This is more likely to happen in dry weather if the plants have not been watered regularly. Pick off the worst affected leaves and spray the remainder with derris or bioresmethrin.

Canker: this is the most serious problem with parsnips. It appears as firm brown or black patches on the shoulder of the root which then becomes soft and rotten. The secondary rotting which follows the initial discolouration is caused by fungi or bacteria, but the reason for the original discolouration is not known. It is most likely, however,

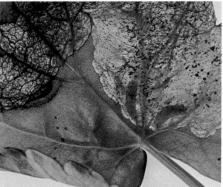

The small maggots of the celery fly burrow into the leaves, causing blisters.

Murphy Chemical

Canker appears as firm patches on the shoulder of the root, which then becomes soft.

Mottled yellow leaves and stunted plants are signs of parsnip virus. Burn affected plants.

that infected roots have been damaged in some way, perhaps by carrot fly, by cracking caused by heavy rain after drought, or by careless hoeing. Because parsnips are not self-healing (as potatoes are, for example), soil-borne fungi and bacteria can enter and rot the root.

The only remedy is better cultivation. Acid soil and over-manuring with unrotted manure are said to encourage canker and these should be avoided. Try, also, later-sown crops, as these are more resistant.

Virus: mottled yellow leaves and stunted plants are signs of parsnip virus. As with all viruses there is no cure. Pull up the affected plants and burn them.

Powdery mildew: parsnip leaves are occasionally attacked by this fungus which appears as a fine white powder on the surface of the leaves. It is most widespread in damp years but even then it does not seriously affect the growth of the plants, and can be ignored.

Downy mildew: downy mildew appears as moist, dark brown or black spots on the leaves but, again, it is not serious.

Leaf spot: a third disease which attacks parsnip leaves is leaf spot which produces small brown spots on the leaves. Again, do not worry. The disease does not do enough damage to merit control measures.

Sclerotina rot: this disease only attacks roots in store, the roots becoming covered with a fluffy, white mould. To prevent rot, only store in a dry, airy place and do not store damaged roots.

GUIDE TO PARSNIP TROUBLES

Symptoms	Probable cause
Small regular holes in the root	Wireworm
White or pale brown blisters on the leaves, leaves shrivelled	Celery fly
Irregular holes in the root sometimes with small whitish grubs inside	Carrot fly
Leaves curling, slightly discoloured, yellowish, and small	Aphids (greenfly)
Reddish brown, dark brown or black patches on the shoulders of the root	Canker
Mottled yellow leaves and markedly stunted growth	Virus
Fine white powder on the surface of the leaves	Powdery mildew
Moist dark brown or black spots on the leaves	Downy mildew
Small brown spots on the leaves	Leaf spot
Roots in store rotten and covered with a white fluffy mould	Sclerotina rot

Potatoes

Solanum tuberosum (fam. *Solanaceae*)
Half-hardy annual.
Sowing to harvesting time: approximately 13
weeks for early varieties; 17–22 weeks for maincrop
varieties.
Size: average tuber diameter 6–10 cm (2½–4″), although
this varies greatly depending on the crop and the variety.
Early potatoes are generally much smaller than maincrop
varieties. Plants grow to about 60 cm (2′) high.
Yield: approximately 7–9 kg (15–20 lb) per 3 m (10′) row.

Potatoes are one of our staple foods, but
in recent years they have become
increasingly expensive. For many home
growers, this in itself is sufficient reason
to try raising their own potatoes, but
there are other benefits too. Some of the
best quality varieties do not 'travel' well
so you will find they are never available
in shops or supermarkets, and the
flavour and texture of early 'new'
potatoes is undoubtedly at its best
straight from the garden.

If you want potatoes all year round,
you will need to grow three different
groups: early, second early and maincrop. The earlier the variety, the faster
the growth and the lower the yield.

Many people will have space to grow
only a limited number of potatoes. In
this case, it is best to sacrifice the
maincrop and grow the earlies, which are
harvested when potatoes are most
expensive in the shops. For a 3 m (10′)
row you will need about 1 kg (2 lb) of
seed potatoes.

To grow a continuous supply for a

family of four throughout the winter and
spring you will need quite a large area of
land—it will be feasible only if you have
an allotment or large garden. The
quantities of seed potato to order are 2 kg
(4½ lb) of earlies, 5 kg (11 lb) of second
earlies, and 2.5 kg (5½ lb) of maincrop *for
each person*. You will need 20 sq m (24 sq
yd) of land for this amount, that is 80 sq
m (96 sq yd) for a family of four.

Suitable site and soil

In a simple rotation system, potatoes are
generally grown with roots and to
precede the cabbage family, which
appreciates the clean, well-turned condition in which this crop leaves the soil.
Potatoes are a good choice for a first crop
on old pasture or grassland that is being
taken into cultivation. As a precaution
against disease, they must not be grown
in the same soil two years in succession.
Remember that tomatoes and night-
shade weeds are members of the same
family as potatoes and can transmit
infection; tomatoes should never be

1. Put the tubers in egg boxes, top upwards, to encourage sprouting.

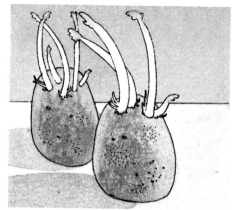

2. Too much warmth or darkness causes shoots unfit for planting.

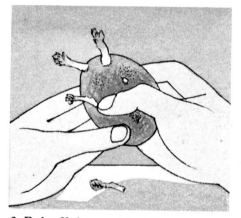

3. Rub off the sprout at the extreme top and all but the two most sturdy.

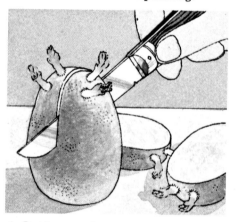

4. Cut large tubers so that each piece has two shoots. Protect cut surfaces.

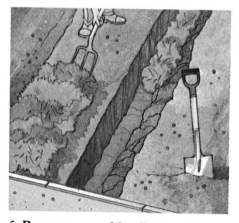

5. Prepare ground by digging over and then manuring before sowing.

6. Make V-shaped furrows 8–15 cm (3-6″) deep for planting sets.

PLANTING THE SETS

7. Put manure where each set is to go, then cover with a thin layer of soil.

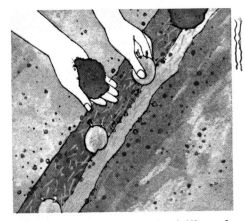

8. Scatter lawn mowings in drills and position sets with tops uppermost.

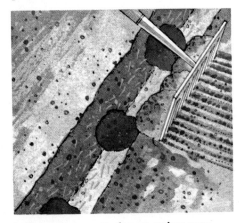

9. Protect sprouts by covering sets with soil by hand, before raking level.

included in the same group of vegetables as potatoes in a rotation system.

The site should be open and not overshadowed by trees, walls or buildings. Potatoes are not particular about soil, but on heavy clay soils choose your varieties carefully. Early varieties prefer light land.

In early winter the ground should be well dug and treated with a moderate amount of rotted manure or compost, but not limed. Lime will encourage attacks of scab, and too much nitrogen will produce growth of the haulm, or stem, at the expense of tubers.

Seaweed, dug into the soil the previous autumn, is an excellent manure. If organic matter is not available, apply a fertilizer made up of 2 parts each by weight of superphosphate and sulphate of ammonia with 1 part of sulphate of potash at the rate of 40 g per sq m ($1\frac{1}{3}$ oz per sq yd). Apply this about two weeks before planting.

Preparing the 'sets'

The 'seed potatoes' from which potatoes are grown are dormant tubers known as 'sets'. These are obtained from vigorous plants before they are fully mature and then exposed to the air for a few days. Potato sets come from disease-free tubers produced on government-certified farms. Never purchase potatoes that do not have a government certificate. Most people buy every year, but it is also safe to grow from tubers of your own crop every other year. Sets should be about the size of a hen's egg and look plump and healthy, but a delivery usually contains some larger ones. These may be divided as described overleaf. It is impossible to get a good crop from poor or diseased sets, so if you are using your own sets be sure they are healthy.

Order seed potatoes in time to begin sprouting towards the end of winter (earlier for early varieties).

Right: flourishing rows of healthy potatoes: a good example of earthing up. Sound cultivation will pay off with a heavy crop.

10. When haulms are 7.5 cm (3″) high, cover them with straw to give protection against damage by frost.

11. Begin earthing-up when the haulms reach 20 cm (8″) to aid production and protect from light.

Put the sets in trays or empty egg-boxes in a light, well-ventilated, frost-proof place. This enables growth to begin before it would be wise to plant outside in spring. The stacking wooden fruit trays that have a short leg sticking upwards at each corner are also ideal for this. Look for the end of the set where the 'eyes' or dormant buds are crowded together—this is the top. Stand them upwards in the trays or egg-boxes and, if there is any risk of frost, cover with newspaper. Chitting, as this process is called, takes about six weeks and gives both earlier and heavier crops.

The earlies should go into sheltered ground at the end of winter, with second earlies and maincrops following at monthly intervals. You can give some earlies a really good start with cloches, but keep the tunnel end closed until all danger of frost is past. Plant when the sprouts on the potato sets you are chitting are 3 cm (1¼″) long. Just before

planting, rub off all except two or three sprouts with your thumb. The one to get rid of first is the sprout at the extreme top, then any that are still white, as the best ones are purplish and, lastly, the least promising of any surplus remaining. Large sets can be cut into pieces, each having at least two strong sprouts. Dust the cut faces with flowers of sulphate or plaster of Paris to check loss of moisture; alternatively, bring the exposed surfaces together and cover with a damp cloth until planting. Take care not to knock off the sprouts.

Planting out

Potato rows should run north to south so that the plants receive the maximum amount of sunshine and do not shade other crops. The rows should be 50 cm (20″) apart for earlies and 75 cm (30″) for the bulkier maincrop plants. This allows for earthing up later on.

Dig V-shaped furrows; the depth will

12. Correct (top) and incorrect (bottom) earthing up. Tubers exposed to light will turn green and poisonous.

13. Spray maincrops against blight in midsummer and again in late summer with Bordeaux mixture.

vary depending on your soil type: from 8 cm (3¼") deep for a heavy soil to 15 cm (6") deep for a light one. Never use a dibber for planting because it is liable to leave an air-space underneath the tuber. For improved yield spread a forkful of manure where each set is to go and throw 3 cm (1½") of soil over it, so that manure and set will not be in direct contact. Scatter lawn mowings thinly in and around the drills before filling them in; this will help prevent attacks of the potato scab fungus.

Place each set in position in the drill, top uppermost, 30 cm (1') apart for earlies and 40 cm (16") for maincrops, covering each with soil by hand to protect the sprouts from damage when refilling the furrow. Rake the soil level along each row.

Care and cultivation

Protection is necessary for all potatoes when there is any risk of frost—as there nearly always is with the earlies. Once the shoots are above the surface, ground or wind frost will burn them black, giving a three-week setback. When they are only a few centimetres high, cover them by drawing up a little soil. When they reach 7.5–10 cm (3–4"), they must be covered with straw, bracken or leafy branches.

Wait until the shoots can be clearly seen before doing any hoeing, and then do not work the hoe too close to them. Start earthing up when the shoots are about 17.5 cm (7") high. The haulms of potato plants are jointed, and the tubers grow out from underground joints in the haulm. Earthing up creates more joints, which means heavier crops.

Earthing up also keeps the tubers well buried so that they will not turn green through exposure to light—green tubers contain a poisonous substance and are dangerous to eat. Several times during the growing period, loosen up the soil

14. Yellowish leaves indicate the crop is ready. Lift with a potato fork which has special tines to avoid damage.

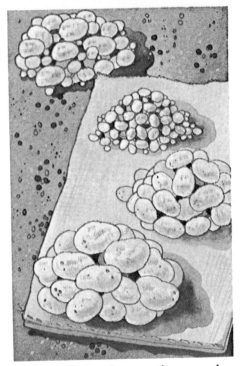

15. Dry off the tubers on the ground, briefly. Clean by hand, discard damaged ones and grade by size.

between the rows and push some up with a draw-hoe on both sides of the haulms, leaving the top 15 cm (6″) uncovered.

Spray against the fungus disease, blight, of maincrops once in midsummer and again in late summer with Bordeaux or Burgundy mixture. These can protect against blight but not cure it. Any flowers that appear during growth should be nipped off.

When growth slows and the haulms turn yellow, the tubers begin to mature. This should happen to all the plants at about the same time and if isolated plants show these signs you must suspect disease—cut their tops down and burn them, although the tubers of these plants may be left in the soil until they are of usable size to be harvested.

Harvesting and storing the crop

Early or 'new' potatoes are eaten immature in early summer, when they are no larger than a pullet's egg.

Carefully lift one or two to see if they are ready for eating; they can be covered up again if they are not. Some people unearth them by hand, pick the tubers they want, and return the soil to let the rest grow on. Dig up the earlies as you need them day by day, because after they are lifted they quickly lose flavour.

A potato fork is a great asset in lifting the crop, as its flat, blunt tines greatly cut down the risk of damaging tubers. Make sure no potatoes or pieces of tuber are left in the ground over winter—they will be a nuisance growing up among the brassicas the next year, and destroy the principle of not growing potatoes in the same soil two years running.

The earlies can go straight into the kitchen as required, but the later crops must be stored. After lifting, let them dry off on the ground for an hour or two, but no longer, before being taken in. Clean off by hand any soil which is sticking to the tubers, discard any that are diseased or damaged, and take the opportunity to pick out any seed potatoes you may require or to do any other kind of grading. Store them in the dark or under cover from light in a dry, frost- and draught-free storeroom. Bags or boxes will do for storing, but put straw under the bags and take precautions against vermin. The potatoes should be inspected once a month, and any rotten ones should be discarded. Also rub off any sprouts.

If you have a lot of potatoes and only a small amount of room, one solution is a clamp raised in a dry open situation out of doors on a thick bed of straw. Heap the potatoes into a ridge on the straw and cover them quickly with more straw, then put some soil on top to keep it in place. After 24 hours' drying cover the straw with 15 cm (6″) of soil, obtained by digging a drainage trench all round the clamp. This is then beaten flat with the spade so it will shed rain. Leave ventilation holes at 1 m (1 yd) intervals along the top, pulling up tufts of straw from below to keep them open. When removing potatoes, inspect those exposed to view before closing the breach. If any are rotten you must remake the clamp. Take the haulms away and burn them; do not use them for compost.

Alternative methods of cultivation

It is not essential to earth up potatoes but the traditional method described is still widely favoured. Cultivation time may be cut by planting the tubers individually along the rows with a trowel (without making a trench) and covering the rows with lengths of black plastic sheeting tucked into slits made in the soil, at both its sides and ends, so as to anchor them. When the shoots start to grow and make bumps in the plastic, make openings with scissors in the form of plus signs to release them. The opaque sheeting conserves moisture, inhibits weeds, and shields the shallow-grown tubers from light. Harvest the potatoes by cutting or rolling back the plastic and lifting them up with a hand fork or potato fork.

Growing under glass

Spring supplies of new potatoes can be produced by planting them in warm frames in mid-winter, either directly in the soil or in pots, but few gardeners have this much frame accommodation. Half bury each upright set in a 20 cm (8″) pot about a third full, and earth them up as they grow. Potatoes can be successfully grown in pots under glass. Fill 20 cm (8″) pots with a good quality compost

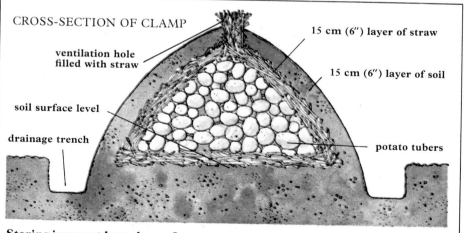

CROSS-SECTION OF CLAMP

15 cm (6″) layer of straw

ventilation hole filled with straw

15 cm (6″) layer of soil

soil surface level

drainage trench

potato tubers

Storing in an outdoor clamp. Inspect potatoes regularly and, if any are rotten, remake the clamp. Potatoes in a well-made clamp should keep several months.

GROWING UNDER PLASTIC SHEETS

1. There is no need to make a trench. Dig holes along the row with a trowel and plant the tubers individually.

2. Cover the rows with lengths of black plastic sheeting. Tuck sheet in slits dug in the soil, at both sides and ends to anchor.

3. When the haulms start to grow and make bumps in the plastic, cut openings in the sheet in the form of plus signs.

4. The sheeting conserves moisture, inhibits weeds, and shields the shallow-grown tubers from the light. Roll back plastic sheeting to harvest. Lift crop with a hand or potato fork.

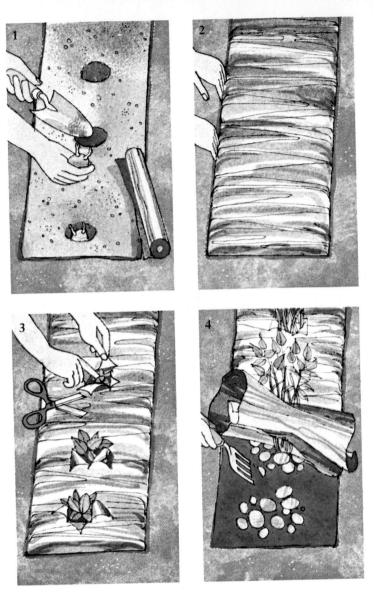

and plant one sprouted tuber in each pot. If you have a heated greenhouse, plant the tubers in late winter and the potatoes will be ready in late spring. If you have an unheated greenhouse or cold frame, expect potatoes in early summer from an early spring planting.

Growing in containers

If your garden is very small, you may want to grow some early potatoes in containers outdoors, or on a patio or balcony. Tubs made from half wine barrels or 30 cm (1′) whalehide containers are the most suitable. Fill with a good quality compost and plant three seed potatoes in each container. If your containers will be indoors, you can plant at any time; if outdoors, late winter or early spring is the best time.

Keep the containers in a warm, sunny place, and bring them indoors if there is a threat of frost. Use a small hoe to earth up the plants exactly as you would if they

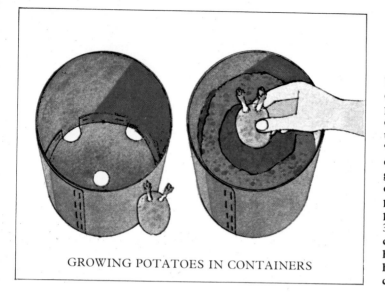

GROWING POTATOES IN CONTAINERS

Yet another way of growing potatoes outdoors is to plant them in 'whalehide' containers. Use good quality compost and plant one seed potato in each 30 cm (1′) container. Use a hand fork when harvesting the crop.

were planted in the ground. Your small crop should be ready for harvesting in about 12 to 14 weeks. Use a hand fork to harvest the tubers. You can expect a yield of about 3 kg (6½ lbs) from a barrel or 1 kg from a whalehide tub.

Exhibition tips

You can grow exhibition-quality potatoes in much the same way as you grow tubers for the table, but with special care and with some differences in cultivation details. As with normal cultivation, sets for sprouting should be about the size of a hen's egg, but they should not be cut into pieces for sprouting. Plant them in early spring at intervals of 60 cm (2′) in drills 60 cm (2′) wide, 15 cm (6″) deep and 90 cm (3′) apart. As well as lining the drills with garden compost or well-rotted manure, place each set on a mixture of old, crumbly manure, sifted peat and leafmould separated from the set by old (but not diseased) potting soil, and cover them with the same mixture. Take care not to let any manure or compost touch the sets.

During cultivation, be extra careful not to tread on the drills when earthing up; remove any weak, spindly shoots as soon as you notice them; keep the healthy stems upright by tying them

carefully to stakes; keep the plants well earthed-up so that the tubers do not turn green; water the plants, using a fine rose on watering can or hose, during dry weather; and be extra vigilant where pests and diseases are concerned.

Growing exhibition potatoes requires a great deal of space, as you will be required to exhibit either six (for a single dish) or twelve (for a collection) regularly-shaped, shallow-eyed, matching tubers: you will be lucky if you find six such tubers in a 9 m (30′) row.

Do not leave the tubers in the ground so long that they are large, heavy and misshapen by the time that you dig them up. Lift them in late summer, handling the tubers very gently. Put them carefully in a container lined with sacks and cover them with dry vermiculite or soft, dry sand. Keep them in a cool place, which should be as dark as possible to prevent the tubers from greening. Near to the time of the show, wash the tubers very carefully (the skins are extremely tender) with a sponge soaked in soapy water. Dry very gently with a soft cloth (pat the tubers; do not rub them), wrap in tissue paper and put them back in the dark until the day of the show. The judges will look for uniformity of size and shape and a clear skin with few eyes.

Pests & Diseases

Potatoes can suffer from many pests and diseases, but the ones given here are those most likely to occur in the garden.

Eelworm: potato root eelworm can be a very serious pest. Eelworm cysts (egg-sacs) can lie dormant in the soil for several years and, when potatoes are planted on infested ground, the larvae attack the tubers, producing potato sickness. Affected plants are stunted and pale green or yellow, they wilt easily and die when immature. Tuber production will be very small. If eelworms are present, there will be tiny dots on the roots, which later become brown. Infected plants and tubers should be destroyed, and infected soil should be put down to grass for eight years. There is no effective method of destroying the cysts. Crop rotation is important in controlling eelworms; never grow potatoes on the same ground two years in a row so otherwise the eelworm population will build up.

Wireworm: these pests can cause much trouble by boring into the potatoes. They are a particular problem in wet summers, and they often occur in freshly dug pasture or on wasteland. If you think wireworms might be a problem, grow

Brian Furner

Potato leaves attacked by the virus leaf roll.

Murphy Chemical Ltd.

Brown patches are a symptom of blight.

early varieties as these are rarely attacked, and lift maincrop potatoes as soon as the tubers mature.

Slugs: slug damage is most likely in wet summers and in heavy, wet soils. Discourage slugs by keeping the garden clear of hiding places and by limiting the use of manure on heavier soils. Use methiocarb or metaldehyde baits to trap them. Early crops are almost never attacked by slugs; damage is usually to maincrop types, and even some of these varieties seem to be immune.

Colorado beetle: colorado beetle is a very destructive pest, fortunately very rare in the UK. The Colorado beetle is a potentially dangerous pest to crops, and its presence must be reported immediately to the government authorities.

Greenfly: greenfly are dangerous to

GUIDE TO POTATO TROUBLES

Symptom	Probable cause
Pale green or yellow leaves	Eelworm Greenfly Virus diseases
Yellowing leaves on blackened stem	Black leg
Brown-black patches on leaves and stems	Potato blight
Curling or rolling leaves	Virus diseases
Large holes in leaves	Colorado beetle
Brown or white dots on roots	Eelworm
Small round holes in tubers	Wireworm
Large holes in tubers	Slugs
Tubers with sunken areas or brown flesh	Potato blight
Large irregular growths on tubers	Wart disease
Rough, discoloured patches on tubers	Scab diseases

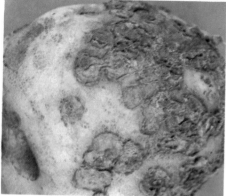

Common scab—but only the skin is damaged.

Slug damage produces large interior holes.

potatoes because they spread virus diseases. Destroy by spraying with derris or resmethrin.

Potato blight: potato blight is one of the most common diseases the home grower encounters. A fungus disease, it is most prevalent in warm, wet weather, but it can occur at any time during the growing season. The disease produces dark brown-black patches on the leaves and stems; infected tubers have sunken areas on the outside with brown flesh underneath. The disease can spread rapidly and destroy the top growth completely in mid-summer.

There are several precautions to take against potato blight. Protect plants by spraying with Bordeaux mixture or mancozeb in early midsummer, and repeat in wet weather according to the manufacturer's instructions. Blighted foliage should be cut and burned, and 10 to 12 days should pass before digging the tubers which are still edible if you catch the disease in its early stages. Blighted potatoes should never be stored.

Potato wart disease: potato wart disease is another fungus disease. Affected tubers produce large irregular growths which look like cauliflowers. Infected plants must be burned, and potatoes should not be planted on the soil for at least ten years. The disease must be notified to the government.

Scab diseases: there are several scab diseases, all caused by fungus, which affect potatoes. Common scab is a superficial disease, affecting the skins of the tubers only, but it makes peeling difficult. It can usually be prevented by lining the drills at planting time with small amounts of lawn mowings. Peelings should be destroyed.

Powdery or corky scab is more serious. It causes round swellings on the tuber skins, which rupture and release a brown, powdery substance. The symptoms can be very severe on wet soil, and the potatoes can be destroyed. The soil can remain contaminated for several years, so avoid growing potatoes on the site of an outbreak.

Black leg: black leg is a bacterial trouble which affects an occasional plant within a crop. The stems blacken at the soil level, the leaves turn yellow and the haulm withers; tubers rot where they are attached to the stem. Dig up infected plants and destroy them.

Virus diseases: leaf-roll, mosaic disease and spraing are all virus infections. Leaf-roll, the most common, is easily recognized by the curling, leathery leaves. The plants are under-sized and the tubers are few and very small. The disease is carried in the tubers, so never save tubers from infected plants for planting out the following year. Mosaic also produces yellow markings on leaves; spraing gives brown lines in the tuber flesh. Avoid these virus infections by planting only certified disease-free seed.

Varieties

First Early

Home Guard: white skin and white flesh; good cropper; excellent value.

Arran Pilot: very popular, high quality, excellent cropping potato; immune to wart disease; rarely affected by scab disease; white-skinned; kidney-shaped; floury and well flavoured.

Ulster Chieftan: one of the earliest croppers; oval-shaped with white flesh.

Di Vernon: deserves to be more popular with gardeners as it is a good cropper and immune to wart disease; kidney-shaped with purple eyes and white flesh.

Duke of York (Midlothian Early): does well in most soils; kidney-shaped potatoes with firm, yellow flesh.

Epicure: an old favourite; one of the best-flavoured varieties for new potatoes; very hardy and suited for cooler parts of the country; round, white-fleshed tubers.

Second Early

Arran Banner: white-skinned, large, round, heavy potatoes; floury; good cropper, particularly on light soils.

Red Craig's Royal: red-skinned tubers of uniform shape and size; does best on heavy soils; high quality; immune to wart disease.

Pentland Lustre: new variety which has

Arran Pilot

Kerr's Pink

King Edward

Pentland Lustre

74

proved very satisfactory; eelworm-resistant; heavy cropper; firm tubers with yellow flesh.

Great Scot: popular type which grows well on most soils; crops and stores well; immune to wart disease; round, white-fleshed tubers are excellent for baking.

Maincrop

Kerr's Pink: pink-skinned; good for areas with high rainfall and/or heavy soil; good cropper.

Desiree: high quality heavy cropper suited to all soil types.

Golden Wonder: considered by many to be the best flavoured potato; excellent type for exhibition; lemon skin and firm, white to yellow flesh; immune to wart disease.

Majestic (Tremendous): most widely grown variety; well-flavoured, kidney-shaped potatoes; suitable for most soils, resistant to blight and immune to wart disease.

King Edward: large, kidney-shaped tubers with pale yellow flesh; does best in medium loam; unfortunately very prone to most potato pests and diseases.

Pentland Crown: recently introduced type bred for immunity to blight and some virus diseases; well-flavoured, oval-shaped tubers with white flesh; heavy cropper.

Brian Furner

Majestic

Harry Smith

Red King Edward

Brian Furner

Arran Banner

Brian Furner

Pentland Crown

Swedes

Brassica napus napobrassica (fam *Cruciferae*)
Hardy biennial
Sowing to harvesting time: 20-24 weeks
Size: 7.5-17.5 cm (3-7″) in diameter, 12.5-17.5 cm (5-7″) long
Yield: 0.5-1 kg (1-2¼lb) per root

Swede is one of the hardiest vegetables, and one of the attractions of growing the crop is its ability to do well without much attention. It can be left in the soil right through the winter and will be wholesome and edible after being frozen solid for weeks.

This cousin of the true turnip originally came from Sweden, and its name is an abbreviation of Swedish turnip. In some northern areas the swede has almost completely superseded the turnip—when a Scotsman talks about turnips he will almost certainly be referring to swedes.

The crop is grown for its large, yellow-fleshed roots. Swedes are hardier, sweeter and milder than turnips, and rarely get woody. The main harvesting difference between swedes and turnips is that swedes are used in winter, while turnips are harvested in summer and autumn. The growing season of the swede is much longer than the turnip's; growing a combination of two vegetables will give you a long season of use.

Although this crop is grown mainly for its edible roots, swedes left in the ground will produce pale green leaves in spring which can be cooked as greens.

Swedes are divided into three groups according to the colour of the upper part of the root: the Purple-tops, the Bronze-tops and the Green-tops. The green varieties are slower to mature than the purple sorts, which are much freer growing and the heaviest croppers. The bronze varieties are intermediate in habit between the two other types. Seeds of Green-top varieties are sometimes difficult to obtain.

Soil preparation

Swedes grow best on fertile medium loam, although with proper soil preparation they will grow well on a wide variety of soils, from light, sandy loams to medium clay.

Swedes, like other members of the brassica family, are subject to club root disease. Club root thrives in acid soil, so

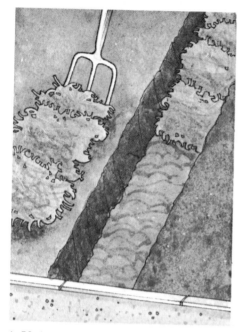

1. If the soil is not fertile, prepare it by digging in plenty of well-rotted manure or garden compost.

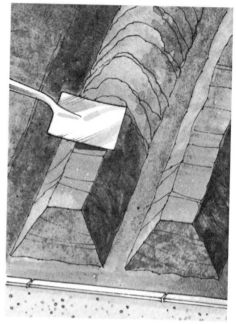

2. In wet areas, prepare rows of ridges 15–20 cm (6–8″) high and sow seeds on ridge tops.

3. Ten days before sowing, apply a compound fertilizer at the rate of 90 g per sq m (3 oz per sq yd).

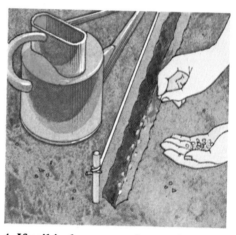

4. If soil is dry, water thoroughly just before sowing; sow seeds thinly and lightly cover with soil.

make sure your soil is between pH 7.0 and 7.3. If the soil is less than 7.0, apply ground limestone at between 0.28 and 1.4 kg per sq m (10 oz and 3 lb per sq yd) depending on acidity.

Provided the soil was well manured for the previous crop, there should be sufficient organic matter for the swede crop. If the soil was not previously manured, dig in well-rotted manure or compost at the rate of one barrowload to 11 sq m (12 sq yd). Do not apply fresh manure or compost, or watery, misshapen roots will result.

1. Three weeks after sowing, or when seedlings are at rough-leaf stage, thin to 15–20 cm (6–8″) apart.

2. Keep down weeds by hoeing between rows and hand weeding between plants.

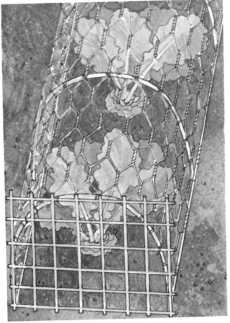

3. Keep the plants well watered until established; mulch with damp peat in very dry weather.

4. Protect the overwintering swedes from attack by pigeons and rabbits with netting or rabbit fencing.

Swedes have long, ridged necks, and mild, orange-yellow flesh. They are hardier than turnips and can remain in the soil right through the winter.

Harry Smith

The amount of fertilizer applied depends on the nature of the soil, but a good basic feed is 90 g per sq m (3 oz per sq yd) of compound fertilizer applied about ten days before sowing and lightly forked in. On chalk soils apply an extra 60 g per sq m (2 oz per sq yd) of superphosphate. On peaty soils, or those which are acid, fork in 60 g per sq m (2 oz per sq yd) of bone meal. Apply these extra fertilizers at the same time as the compound fertilizer.

When preparing the ground, make sure you get rid of all weeds, particularly the perennial ones, such as couch grass and thistles.

If you live in an area of high rainfall, it is best to grow swedes on ridges. It is hard to precisely define high rainfall, but if you get more than 60 cm (24″) of rain per year, you would do better to grow the crop on ridges. Make ridges 15-20 cm (6-8″) high, and between 60-67 cm (24-27″) from centre to centre (see diagram). Ridges are better drained in winter,

when the ground tends to get water-logged. Fine soil will gradually fall down to the bottom of the trench between the ridges and the roots will grow through into this.

In lower rainfall areas grow swedes on the flat, as ridges would tend to dry out in the summer. For the same reason, do not make ridges if your soil is very sandy or free-draining.

Firm the ground before sowing, whether on ridges or on the flat. Do not attempt to firm the ground if it is too wet, or the soil will become compacted and lose its friable quality.

Seed sowing

The time for seed sowing varies according to local conditions. In Britain, sowing should take place in late spring in the north, early summer in the midlands, and mid-summer in the south and southeast. The temperature required for germination is over 7° C (45° F) and less than 37°C (95°F). By sowing late in the

79

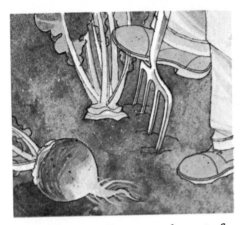

To harvest, gently ease swedes out of ground with a garden fork.

Top and tail the swedes before storing for future use.

season in warmer areas, the plants will be less subject to the worst summer heat, drought and mildews. A last sowing in late summer will provide greens for use the following spring.

If you are growing swedes on ridges, sow the seed as soon as possible after the ridges are prepared. If the soil is dry, water the drills right before sowing. The rows should be about 67 cm (27″) apart; rows on the flat should be 45 cm (18″) apart. Sow the seeds thinly, at a depth of 2 cm ($\frac{3}{4}$″) on light soils, or 1.25 cm ($\frac{1}{2}$″) on heavier ground.

Care and cultivation

The seeds take between seven and twelve days to germinate. Thinning takes place about three weeks after sowing, when the seedlings are at the rough-leaf stage. Do not attempt to transplant the thinnings as, once disturbed, they will not grow. The final spacing of the young plants should be 25-30 cm (10-12″) apart in the rows.

Keep the young plants well watered until established. Cultivate the ground to kill weeds, being careful not to damage the young swede roots. Do not hoe too deeply; lightly loosening the soil surface will create a dust mulch which helps to conserve the moisture below. If the weather is dry, mulch with damp peat,

Storing in a clamp: dig drainage trench; place swedes on a layer of straw.

working it up and over the tops of any protruding roots.

Harvesting and storing

Although swedes may be large enough to use in early autumn, they are often left in the ground until all the summer vegetables have been harvested and frost has set in. They can be pulled as required through the winter, as long as the ground is soft enough to dig. A touch of frost improves the flavour of swedes. The over-wintering roots are, however, vulnerable to attack by rabbits and pigeons, so make sure they are ade-

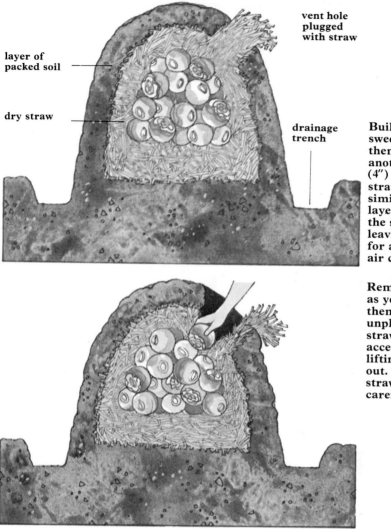

layer of
packed soil

dry straw

vent hole
plugged
with straw

drainage
trench

Build up heap of
swedes. Cover
them with
another 10 cm
(4") layer of
straw. Put a
similar depth
layer of soil over
the straw,
leaving a vent
for access and
air circulation.

Remove swedes
as you need
them by
unplugging the
straw in the
access vent and
lifting the roots
out. Replace the
straw plug
carefully.

quately protected with nets or rabbit fencing. Alternatively, you can leave them in the ground until spring, when they will produce leaves which can be cut and used as greens.

In the south winters are rarely severe, and you can usually leave the roots in the ground until you are ready to use them. Lift them systematically; do not pull the biggest ones first. You will then have feasible areas of cleared ground to dig over before winter sets in and any swedes left in the ground for spring greens will be grouped together.

An outdoor crop of spring greens is harvested by cutting off the tufts of leaves at the neck as you require them.

If you live in a cold area, have a good supply of roots and some storage space, you can lift some of the swedes and store them in boxes or an outdoor clamp to ensure that you will have a supply when the rest of the crop is frozen hard in the ground.

Lifting the crop can begin in late autumn. Choose a mild day, and gently ease the roots out of the ground with a garden fork. If you are storing them for future use, top and tail them. Removing the leaves and root tails makes them

PRODUCING BLANCHED STEMS

1. Dig up swedes in late autumn; cut back neck and root, plant in box filled with soil or peat. Water well and store in dark place.

2. Cut blanched shoots when they are 20 cm (8″) long.

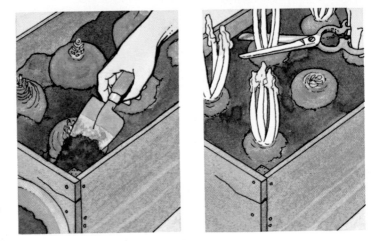

easier to store, and helps prevent rot.

To store them indoors, pack the swedes in layers in a box, and cover them with fine sand. They can also be stored loose in a sack. Whichever method of indoor storing you use, make sure you keep them cool, preferably at a temperature of 0-4° C (32-40° F). Be on the look out for vermin, such as mice or rats; if you see any, put down poison or set traps.

To make a clamp for outside storage in cold districts, select a plot of ground not subject to waterlogging, and clear it of all rubbish. Lay a 10 cm (4″) layer of clean dry straw on the soil, and put the swedes on top. Cover them with another 10 cm (4″) layer of straw. Then place a covering of soil, 7.5-10 cm (3-4″) deep, over the straw, leaving an access vent, or more than one in larger clamps. A shallow trench around the clamp will have been formed by excavating the soil. On heavy soils water would collect in the trench, so build up a pathway at the original soil level to the clamp, to avoid having to walk through the water.

Producing blanched stems
You can induce swede roots to produce blanched stems, like chicory, which are excellent in winter salads or as a cooked vegetable. Dig up medium-sized roots in late autumn or early winter, after a few winter frosts. You do not need the best

roots for forcing, small or misshapen ones will do just as well. Cut off all top growth above 2.5 cm (1″); shorten back the neck and root tail to the swollen root base. These swedes should be about 10 cm (4″) in diameter, and 17.5 cm (7″) long. Then fill boxes with friable soil or peat to a depth of 2.5 cm (1″). Press the roots gently into the soil with a space of about 2.5 cm (1″) between them. Continue filling the spaces between the swedes with peat or soil until the soil is level with the neck of the swedes. Water them well, and keep them in a dark place, with a temperature of 13-15° C (55-60° F). Cut the blanched shoots when they are about 20 cm (8″) long.

Exhibition tips
Swedes for exhibition should be medium-sized, clear-skinned, solid and shapely, with small taproots. Prior to the show, lift the roots carefully, so they are not damaged. Place them on wet sacking in a cool place, and keep them covered. Wash the swedes in cold water, sponging off any soil which is sticking to the root. Cut off any whiskery side roots and dead outer foliage. Then cut back the remaining foliage to 10 cm (4″) and tie with green twine. Usually three or six swedes are shown; these should be displayed on a plate with the roots facing frontwards. Swedes are often used in displays of mixed vegetables.

G. E. Hyde

Harry Smith

Varieties

Purple-top: Excellent for eating and for winter storage.

Chignecto: bred for its resistance to club root disease; a first-class table swede, having a fine neck with perfectly round root of the Purple-top type.

Mancunian: greenish-bronze topped root with solid yellow flesh. Excellent keeping, though slower growing than Purple-top varieties.

Western Perfection: a very good quick-growing Purple-top sort with yellow fleshed root; almost neckless; splendid for eating young and stores well.

Acme: excellent for table use; sweet yellow flesh, Purple-top variety.

Above left: Typical Bronze Top variety

Above: Chignecto

Left: Purple Top

Brian Furner

Pests & Diseases

Common sense, clean cultivation and crop rotation will do much to minimize the harmful effects of pests and diseases. The four main troubles which commonly occur in swede crops are club root, also known as 'Finger and Toe', downy mildew, turnip flea beetle, and gall weevil. These will also affect other members of the brassica family; club root, which is particularly destructive, may persist in the soil for many years.

Flea beetle: these are usually most destructive at the seedling stage and occur mainly in dry weather. They eat small round holes in the leaves; in severe cases the plants may be entirely defoliated. Treat the seed before sowing with gamma-HCH, and dust it on the seedlings when they appear, or use derris on the plants.

Aphids: greenfly, blackfly or cabbage aphids will occasionally appear during hot, dry weather. They form large colonies on the under and upper surfaces of the leaves which causes the leaves to curl; stems may also become twisted and distorted. Control them with malathion or derris sprays.

Shell photo

Gall weevil maggots occupy the cavities in the swellings on swede roots.

Ministry of Agriculture, Fisheries and Food

Club root is a very serious fungal disease, causing swollen, foul smelling inedible roots.

Murphy Chemicals Ltd.

Turnip flea beetle damage; the beetles can defoliate young plants.

Gall weevil: white maggots attack the roots, causing round swellings to appear on the upper part of the roots. Treat the seed with gamma-HCH (BHC).

Wireworms: these shiny yellow worms occasionally tunnel into the roots; they usually occur on ground freshly turned over after grass. Gamma-HCH (BHC) dust raked in before sowing will help to minimize the attacks.

Slugs and snails: these pests do twofold damage. They eat the leaves and roots, and the holes they make allow root rotting disease organisms to enter. Control slugs and snails with any proprietary bait.

Club root disease: this fungus attacks not only other brassicas, but most members of the *Cruciferae* family. The symptoms of the disease are stunted and weak plants having swollen roots. The infected roots are gnarled and galled, slimy, rotten, and foul smelling. Prevention is the best defence. Ensure that ground is not too acid before sowing, as club root thrives in acid soils. It is prevalent on badly-drained soils; make sure drainage problems have been corrected before sowing. Do not grow swedes on land which has grown any brassicas in the last two years. Lastly, avoid using manure or compost containing infected roots or leaves.

Liming the soil will help control the disease; sprinkle hydrated lime at the rate of 6 kg to every 30 sq m (14 lb every 30 sq yds). Sprinkle 4% calomel dust in the seed drills before sowing, at the rate of 30 g per 1.5 m (1 oz per 5′ run).

Downy mildew: the first sign of this infection is the appearance of greyish-white patches on the leaves, generally on the undersurface, followed by wilting and yellowing. Spray the plants with zineb.

Powdery mildew: this appears as whitish powdery patches on the leaves. Pick off affected leaves and spray plants with dinocap.

Root rots: dry rot, or phoma rot, occurs as a brown, sunken, elongated canker-like areas on the side of the roots. Prevention is again the main control of this problem. Eliminate slugs and snails and avoid using manure or compost containing infected roots. Use the same preventive measures against soft rot, which causes brown or grey mottling and eventual softness and sliminess of the root.

Wirestem: this causes damping off of seedlings, but stem bases of older plants may be attacked; the stems turn brown, shrink and break off easily. It is not necessarily fatal to the crop, but infected plants will be stunted. Prevent wirestem by treating soil with quintozene dust at sowing time.

GUIDE TO SWEDE TROUBLES

Symptoms	*Probable Cause*
Curled leaves, twisted stems with colonies of green, black or bluish insects on leaves and stems.	Aphids
Small round holes in leaves of seedlings or plants.	Flea beetles
Swellings, on upper part of roots, containing white maggots.	Gall weevil
Slime trails, holed leaves, stalks and roots.	Slugs and snails
Shiny, yellow worms and tunnels in the roots.	Wireworms
Weak, sickly plants with swollen, galled, bad smelling and rotting roots.	Club root disease
Greyish-white downy patch or leaves turning yellow and wilting.	Downy mildew
Whitish powdery patches on leaves.	Powdery mildew
Brown, sunken elongated canker-like areas on the side of the roots.	Phoma rot
Grey or brown mottled areas, some being soft and slimy in the advanced stages.	Soft rot
Seedling stems constricted and brittle, some falling over and dying.	Wirestem Damping off

Turnips

Brassica rapa (fam. *Cruciferae*)
Hardy biennial
Sowing to harvesting time: maincrop 10–12 weeks: early crops 6–8 weeks
Size: maincrop roots average 7.5–10 cm (3–4″) across, but can grow much larger; early crop roots about 4 cm (1½″); leaves to 30 cm (12″) long.
Yield: maincrop roots average 260–480 g (½–1 lb), but can be much heavier; early crop roots weigh about 90 g (3 oz).

Turnips are quick and easy to grow, and their swollen white roots provide a delicate flavour when used in stews or casseroles, or served on their own as a vegetable. Although often thought of as an autumn and winter crop, turnips are much more versatile. By selecting your varieties carefully to suit the season, and by meeting their few cultivation needs, you can extend cropping over many months.

In the annual garden cycle, turnips can be regarded as three distinct crops. Early turnips are those which are ready to harvest as quite small roots from mid-spring to early summer. They may be grown outdoors on a hotbed in a frame, or started in a greenhouse or outdoors under cloches. These quick-growing tender varities have long or spherical roots, white flesh and white skin, sometimes with purple or red shading. They are French or Italian in origin and are not hardy. Because they are so quick growing, they make excellent catch crops.

Maincrop turnips are sown in the summer to produce roots 7.5–10 cm (3–4″) in diameter in autumn. In mild areas they can be lifted as needed through the winter; in colder areas they are lifted all at once in late autumn and stored. These larger, hardier varieties were developed in England and Scotland to withstand winter weather. They are usually round and white fleshed, and either white or white and green skinned. There is a yellow fleshed variety, which is a mutation, or 'sport', of the white fleshed turnip. It is used for maincrops, and its flesh is considered by many to be superior in taste to most of the other turnip varieties.

Finally, you can grow turnips in spring or autumn for their leaves, which are cooked like cabbage and are rich in vitamin C and iron. The leaves can either be harvested as thinnings, before the roots have fully formed, or the roots can be left in the ground over winter to produce a continuous supply of spring greens.

Turnips are one of the easiest garden vegetables to grow; both leaves and roots are edible.

Suitable site and soil

Turnips require an open, sunny position. If grown in the shade of trees, they will produce foliage rather than roots. For early turnips, the site should have some shelter from north and east winds.

Although turnips will grow on a wide variety of soils, the main requirement is that the soil is moisture retentive; rich sandy loams are ideal. Turnips like calcium and are grown extensively on chalk and limestone soils; they also need a soil well supplied with phosphates.

Turnips grow best on a soil which has been manured for a previous crop, such as potatoes. If the site has not been previously prepared, dig the soil over in autumn or early winter. If it is dry or heavy, dig in plenty of well-rotted manure or compost to improve moisture

retention and drainage. If you are digging in manure, bury it deeply or the roots will be mis-shapen and earthy tasting. Unless the soil is chalky or limey, apply a top dressing of carbonate of lime to ensure that the soil is neutral to slightly alkaline. Allow two months to elapse between manuring and liming, otherwise the nutrients in the manure will be released into the air.

Sowing

In theory, the gardener can grow a succession of crops from early spring until late autumn. Two crops are more practical, an early one harvested in spring or early summer, and a maincrop harvested in autumn and stored through the winter. An intermediate crop would coincide with the main summer veget-

1. Begin digging the soil in autumn or early winter; work in plenty of well rotted manure or garden compost.

2. Unless your soil is chalky or limey, apply a top dressing of carbonate of lime to make the soil neutral in pH.

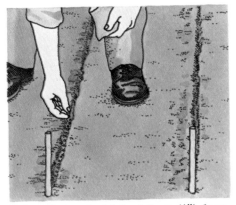

3. Sow the seeds thinly, 1.2 cm ($\frac{1}{2}''$) deep, in drills 30-40 cm (12-16") apart; any extra seed can be stored for later use.

ables, and any seed sown in late spring for harvesting in summer would quickly bolt under hot, dry weather conditions.

For the first sowing, choose an early, quick growing variety and start under glass or cloches. For maincrop turnips, sow in mid to late summer, again selecting a suitable variety. A final sowing in early autumn will provide turnip tops in spring, with a cutting, if required, in late autumn, within a few weeks of sowing.

The early varieties generally have white roots. A succession is provided by more white varieties, by white turnips with red or purple tops, and lastly by golden ones. Green top white varieties are among the hardiest and best for overwintering to supply early spring greens.

Sow the seeds thinly, 1.5 cm ($\frac{1}{2}''$) deep, in drills 30–40 cm (12–16") apart; 7 g ($\frac{1}{4}$ oz) of seed is enough to sow a 9m (30') row; if you have more seed than you need, you can store it; the seed remains viable for three years.

Thin the seedlings as soon as they are large enough to handle to a distance of 5 cm (2") apart. Pairs of seedlings occasionally grow very close together and appear as one seedling, so thin carefully. Thin early crops and turnips grown for greens to a final spacing of 15 cm (6") between plants. Turnips grown as maincrop should be thinned to a distance of 23–30 cm (9–12") apart. If you spread the second thinning over a period of several weeks, you can use the thinnings as spring greens. The sowing to germinating period varies according to soil warmth, but in reasonably warm weather germination is rapid and can take less than a week. Like most other root crops, turnips do not transplant well.

Cultivation and care

The cultivation needs of turnips are moderate and fairly basic. For early sowings in the open, protect the plants with cloches if the weather turns cold. Turnip seedlings are particularly vul-

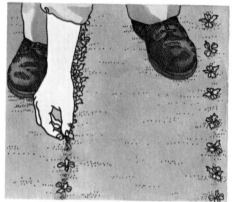

1. The first thinning takes place when the seedlings are large enough to handle; thin to 5 cm (2") apart.

2. Thin again to 15 cm (6") apart for early crops and those for greens; space maincrops 22-30 cm (9-12") apart.

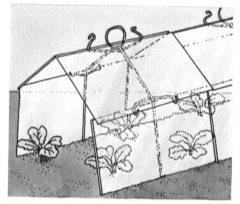

3. For early sowings in open ground, protect the plants with cloches if the weather turns cold or frost threatens.

4. Dust the young plants with derris as a precaution against turnip flea beetle; reapply as necessary.

5. The turnips should receive a steady supply of water while growing, or they will bolt without forming roots.

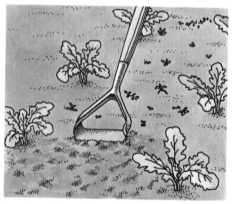

6. Keep the soil well hoed, being careful nor to damage the roots; this controls weeds and keeps soil aerated.

1. **Pick early turnips when they are the size of a tennis ball; maincrops can be left in the ground until needed.**

2. **Pull turnip tops when they are 15 cm (6″) high; do not pull more than two leaves from a plant at one time.**

3. **In cold areas, lift maincrops in late autumn for storing; place roots in boxes between layers of peat or sand.**

nerable to attack by flea beetle, so dust the drills with derris as soon as the seedlings emerge and continue dusting with derris as necessary.

Spring turnips should be grown as quickly as possible, without any checks. This means there must be a constant and steady supply of water. If the turnips grow in dry soil, they will either run to seed without forming roots or else the roots will be coarse, stringy and unpleasant. On the other hand, if the turnips are watered heavily following a long dry spell, their roots will split.

Keep the soil well hoed, being careful not to damage the roots. This helps to control weeds and also keeps the soil aerated.

Harvesting and aftercare

Turnips are best when grown quickly and harvested while still young and tender. Pull spring turnips when they are about the size of a tennis ball, and cut the leaves off close to the root. The spring crop of leaves may be picked. or cut at any time after they are about 10–15 cm (4–6″) high. Most of the turnip varieties which are grown for pulling when young are not frost hardy, and if you make a late sowing, they should be out of the ground before the onset of hard frost.

Hardier winter varieties can withstand a moderately mild winter, and in the south of England may be pulled as required. Alternatively, if you live in a cold, wet area, or where the ground is likely to be frozen hard, lift the turnips for storage in clamps or boxes until needed. Begin harvesting for storing when the outer leaves show signs of ripening in late autumn; leave about 2.5 cm (1″) of leaf stalk attached to the roots. If storing them in a box, pack the roots between layers of dry peat or sand, and store in a cool place where they will keep until early spring.

Lift the roots systematically for immediate use or storing; do not pull the biggest ones first. In this way you will have a feasible area of cleared ground to

Turnip leaves, or 'tops', are rich in vitamin C and iron; cook them like spring greens.

dig over before planting the next crop; any turnips left in the ground for spring greens will be grouped in one place. These spring greens will be particularly useful at a time of the year when cabbages are scarce. Do not pick all the leaves off one plant, or it will stop producing new growth. Pick just one or two leaves from each one, so the plants will continue producing fresh foliage. As soon as the plants form flowerheads, however, scrap them, as the leaves will be bitter and unpleasant tasting.

To avoid pests and diseases, clear away all surplus roots and the remains of vegetation after harvesting and take them to the compost heap. If you have had serious trouble with pests or diseases, do not risk spreading them through the compost heap; dig up and burn all debris instead.

Growing turnips under glass

Turnips may be produced very early in the season if you grow them under glass. They will not stand hard forcing, however, so if you grow them in a frame on a hotbed use gentle bottom heat only. Fermenting manure or leaf litter covered with 15 cm (6″) of fine soil should be adequate. Insert the seeds, two or three together, in holes about 12.5 cm (5″) apart in mid to late winter. Thin to one seedling per hole when the seedlings are large enough to handle. The bed should be covered by sacks or mats to help retain the heat until the seeds have germinated; remove the sacks once the seedlings

1. For growing in a frame on a hotbed use gentle heat only; cover a layer of manure or leaf litter with fine soil.

2. Insert seeds, in groups of two or three, in holes 12.5-15 cm (5-6″) apart, in mid to late winter.

3. Cover the lights with sacks or mats to help retain heat until seeds have germinated; then remove the sacks.

appear. Allow plenty of air to circulate round the plants after this, and water every day. It should be possible to harvest the crop within four to eight weeks of sowing.

Alternatively, if you want early turnips without using a hotbed, you can grow them under cloches in early spring. Keep them covered with the cloches and thin the seedlings so they are 15 cm (6″) apart. You should have tender roots for pulling in about six weeks. Turnips left in the soil over winter to produce spring greens may also need cloche protection if the weather turns very cold.

Exhibition tips

It is risky to try to time a single sowing of turnips to be ready for a show date, because unforeseen changes in weather can retard or advance the growth considerably. Make several small sowings, nine, ten and eleven weeks before the show, and select the best roots for exhibition. Six turnips is the usual number shown in single dishes, and ten turnips in a collection of vegetables.

The globe turnips should be a little larger than a tennis ball, and as uniform in size, weight, and general appearance as possible. Globe varieties should be perfectly round, without any taper to the tap root. Long varieties should be 3.7 cm (1½″) in diameter, and 12–15 cm (5–6″) long. For all varieties, the judges will look for clear skins and symmetrical, solid roots, with small tap roots.

Lift the roots carefully with a fork, and put them in wet sacking so they do not dry out. Wash any soil off carefully with cold water and a sponge; do not scrub them or the skin will be damaged. Remove the small outer leaf stems entirely, and cut the leaves away so that 12 cm (5″) of leaf stem remains. Trim away any small root hairs from the tap root with a sharp knife.

The roots can be displayed in a circular basket, on a flat plate or board, or hung from wire cones; try to make the display as pleasing and attractive as possible.

Varieties

Early

Early Six Weeks (Early White Stone): fast, first class white globe turnip; early cropper and sweet flavoured; good for growing under glass.

Tokyo Cross (F_1 hybrid): globe shaped roots; very quick growing, ready five weeks from sowing; well flavoured, uniform crops.

Jersey Navet: cylindrical shaped, white fleshed variety; excellent for cold frames or cloches for early crops, or can be sown in open for maincrops.

Golden Perfection: nearly flat golden skinned roots, small to medium sized; tender flesh.

White Milan: very early turnip, excellent for growing under frames or cloches; dwarf, compact roots, flat shaped and medium sized.

Sprinter: early selection of *Purple Top Milan*, but slightly smaller; suitable for growing either under glass or outdoors in the open ground.

Purple Top Milan: white variety with purple top; very early cropper; distinctive, heart-shaped leaves.

Red Globe: round, medium sized roots; white flesh, red and white skin.

Snowball: early variety, quick growing; well formed, round white roots; can be cooked or grated raw; suitable for table and exhibition work.

Brian Furner

Jersey Navet

Brian Furner

Golden Perfection

Brian Furner

Purple Top Milan

Pat Brindley

Red Globe

Snowball

Green-top White

Maincrop
Golden Ball: dwarf and compact; tender yellow flesh; hardier than white-fleshed turnips and lasts well in open; best variety for autumn sowing; flavour only moderate.

Green-top White: round variety, with half green, half white, skin; leaves used as spring greens; heavy cropper; well-flavoured roots.

Manchester Market: excellent green-topped, globe variety; mild flavour; especially recommended for winter use as a table variety.

Pests & Diseases

Club root disease (finger and toe): this is one of the most serious fungal diseases affecting members of the *Cruciferae* family, mainly brassicas; turnip crops can be completely destroyed by severe infections of club root. Yellow fleshed varieties have slightly more resistance to club root than white fleshed varieties. The above ground symptoms are stunted and weak plants with wilted greyish leaves. The roots, when dug up, will appear gnarled and galled, slimy, rotten and foul smelling. Once a soil is infected with club root, it is a lengthy process to eradicate the fungus completely; it is better to try to prevent an attack of club root than to cure it. Because club root is associated with acid soils, ensure that the ground is not too acid before sowing. Correct any drainage problems at this time as well, as plants grown on waterlogged soil are particularly vulnerable. To protect seedlings, sprinkle calomel dust, used according to manufacturer's instructions, in the seed drills before sowing.

Make sure you practice crop rotation, and do not grow turnips on land which has grown any brassicas in the last two years. Lastly, dig up and burn any infected plants as soon as you see them; do not put them on the compost heap or the infection is likely to spread.

Liming the soil will help control the disease; sprinkle hydrated lime at the rate of 6 kg to every 30 sq m (14 lb every 30 sq yds).

Dry rot: although swedes are usually more vulnerable to dry rot than turnips, the latter are sometimes infected. The symptoms of dry rot are brown, sunken, canker-like areas on the roots. Prevention is again the best method of controlling the infection. Keep your garden free of slugs and snails, as they cause the wounds through which dry rot enters the roots. Avoid using manures of composts containing pieces of infected roots or leaves. Destroy any infected roots immediately.

This leaf shows the damage done by flea beetle; in severe cases it may be skeletonized.

Wounds made on the leaves and roots by slugs allow infections like soft rot to attack.

Soft rot: this bacterial infection causes brown or grey mottling and eventual softness in the inner root, although the outer skin may remain firm. As with dry rot, the infection usually enters the root through a wound, perhaps from hoe or insect damage. It is also likely to occur where the roots are stored in damp conditions. Dig up and destroy any infected plants, make sure your garden is pest free, and avoid hoeing. Too heavy liming can predispose plants to this trouble, so try to avoid this condition.

Powdery mildew: this mildew is most likely to occur in dry summers. The symptoms are white powdery patches on the leaves. The best precaution is to make sure your plants do not run short of water in dry spells. If powdery mildew does appear, pick off and burn infected leaves and spray the remaining leaves with dinocap.

Brown heart (Raan): the symptoms of this physiological disorder, which is due to boron deficiency, do not appear until the turnip roots are cut open. The plants will show grey or brown areas in the bottom half of the root; the flesh will be bitter, stringy and unpleasant to eat. Brown heart is sometimes associated with very dry soil conditions; if your soil is very free draining, make sure you dig in enough humus when preparing the

site to make the soil moisture retentive. Excessive liming can also cause brown heart, as it makes the boron in the soil unavailable to the plants. Mulching the soil with well rotted compost and digging in manure is the safest method of correcting this deficiency.

GUIDE TO TURNIP TROUBLES

Symptom	Probable cause
Wilted grey leaves, roots mis-shapen, slimy and rotten	Club root
Brown, sunken, canker-like areas on roots	Dry rot
Brown or grey mottling in inner root	Soft rot
White powdery patches on leaves	Powdery mildew
Grey or brown areas in bottom half of root	Brown heart (Raan)
Pale grey patches on undersides of leaves	Downy mildew
Base of stem shrivels and turns brown	Wirestem
Small round holes in leaves	Flea beetle
Galls in roots containing white maggots	Gall weevil
Leaves and roots eaten	Slugs and snails
Tunnels in roots	Wireworm

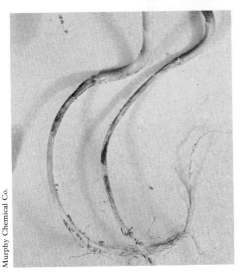

Murphy Chemical Co.

George Hyde

Wireworm: this pest is most troublesome on soil freshly turned over from grass.

Wirestem causes brown, hardened and shrivelled stems; plants will not crop well.

Downy mildew: the first sign of this infection is the appearance of greyish white patches on the undersurfaces of the leaves; seedlings are most likely to be infected. Eventually infected leaves wilt, turn yellow and die. Remove and destroy infected leaves, and spray the remainder with zineb.

Wirestem: this infection causes damping off in seedlings, but older plants may also be infected. Plants infected with this fungal disease will have stems which shrivel, narrow, turn brown and toughen. Although not necessarily fatal, diseased plants will be stunted and poor croppers. Prevent damping off and wirestem by treating the soil with quintozene dust at sowing time, or with a thorough watering of Cheshunt compound.

Flea beetle: this is the most serious pest you are likely to encounter with turnip crops. The most severe attacks occur in hot dry weather, when the plants may be entirely defoliated. The main symptom is small round holes in the leaves; eventually the holes may join up and the leaf skeletonized. Seeds treated with gamma HCH before sowing are less vulnerable to attack. As a further precaution, dust the seedlings as soon as they appear with derris, and repeat if you see holes in the leaves.

Gall weevil: the symptoms of infestation by gall weevil are sometimes confused with those of club root, as in both cases swollen disfigured roots occur. If the suspect roots are cut open and galls are found containing white maggots, then gall weevil is the cause. It is much less serious than club root; the best precaution against gall weevil is to treat the soil with gamma HCH prior to sowing; destroy infected plants.

Slugs and snails: besides damaging turnip crops by feeding on the leaves and roots, the open wounds they make allow more serious secondary infections, such as soft rot and dry rot, to attack the plant. Keep your garden free from debris and litter where snails can hide during the day. Trap slugs in piles of old vegetable matter; inspect the traps daily and remove and destroy any slugs you find. Alternatively, control them with a proprietary slug bait used according to manufacturers' instructions.

Wireworms: these shiny yellow worms are only likely to be a problem on soil freshly turned over after grass; land that has been cultivated for any length of time is usually free from wireworm. The symptoms of wireworm attacks are tunnels through turnip roots; gamma HCH dust raked in before sowing will help to minimize the attacks.